UPGRADE
Active Revision

WORKBOOK

REVISE
AQA GCSE
ENGLISH
LANGUAGE

PRACTICE PAPERS

Beverley Emm

T0346863

OXFORD
UNIVERSITY PRESS

Great Clarendon Street, Oxford, OX2 6DP, United Kingdom

Oxford University Press is a department of the University of Oxford.
It furthers the University's objective of excellence in research, scholarship, and
education by publishing worldwide. Oxford is a registered trade mark of Oxford
University Press in the UK and in certain other countries

British Library Cataloguing in Publication Data

Data available

ISBN 978-1-38-200653-8

10 9 8 7 6 5 4 3 2

Printed in India by Multivista Global Pvt. Ltd

Acknowledgements
The publisher and authors would like to thank the following for permission to use
photographs and other copyright material:

Cover: Heidi's Pics/Shutterstock. Photos: **p9:** Craig Lovell/Eagle Visions Photography/
Alamy Stock Photo; **p37:** Patricia Phillips/Stockimo/Alamy Stock Photo; **p62:**
George Munday/Alamy Stock Photo; **p64:** Newspaper image © The British Library
Board. All rights reserved. With thanks to The British Newspaper Archive (www.
britishnewspaperarchive.co.uk).; **p92:** Cotswolds Photo Library/Alamy Stock Photo;
p94: Dave Head/Shutterstock.

Every effort has been made to contact copyright holders of material reproduced in
this book. Any omissions will be rectified in subsequent printings if notice is given to
the publisher.

The author and publisher are grateful for permission to include extracts from the
following copyright material:

Gavin Bell: 'Through the Pyrenees on the Little Yellow Train', *Daily Telegraph*,
28 March 2016, copyright © Telegraph Media Group Ltd 2016, used by permission
of TMG.

Rachel Campbell-Johnston: *The Child's Elephant's* (David Fickling Books, 2013),
copyright © Rachel Campbell-Johnston 2013, used by permission of The Random
House Group Ltd.

Adèle Geras: *Facing the Light* (Orion, 2013), copyright © Adèle Geras 2003, used by
permission of Peters Fraser & Dunlop (www.petersfraserdunlop.com) on behalf of
Adèle Geras (Loose Ships Ltd).

Robert Macfarlane: *The Old Ways A Journey on Foot* (Hamish Hamilton, 2012), copyright
© Robert Macfarlane 2012, used by permission of Penguin Books Ltd

Although we have made every effort to trace and contact all copyright holders before
publication. If notified, the publisher will rectify any errors or omissions at the
earliest opportunity.

Contents

Introduction

AQA GCSE English Language: specification overview

The grade you receive at the end of your AQA GCSE English Language course is entirely based on your performance in two exam papers.

The following provides a summary of how you will be assessed.

Questions and marks	Assessment Objectives
Paper 1: Explorations in creative reading and writing Section A: Reading Exam text: • One unseen prose fiction text Exam questions and marks: • One short form question (1 x 4 marks) • Two longer form questions (2 x 8 marks) • One extended question (1 x 20 marks) Section B: Writing Descriptive or narrative writing Exam question and marks: • One extended writing question (24 marks for Content and Organisation, 16 marks for Technical Accuracy)	Reading: • AO1 • AO2 • AO4 Writing: • AO5 • AO6
Paper 2: Writers' viewpoints and perspectives Section A: Reading Exam text: • One unseen non-fiction text and one unseen literary non-fiction text Exam questions and marks: • One short form question (1 x 4 marks) • Two longer form questions (1 x 8 marks and 1 x 12 marks) • One extended question (1 x 16 marks) Section B: Writing Writing to present a viewpoint Exam question and marks: • One extended writing question (24 marks for Content and Organisation, 16 marks for Technical Accuracy)	Reading: • AO1 • AO2 • AO3 Writing: • AO5 • AO6

Assessment Objectives	
AO1	• Identify and interpret explicit and implicit information and ideas. • Select and synthesise evidence from different texts.
AO2	Explain, comment on and analyse how writers use language and structure to achieve effects and influence readers, using relevant subject terminology to support their views.
AO3	Compare writers' ideas and perspectives, as well as how these are conveyed, across two or more texts.
AO4	Evaluate texts critically and support this with appropriate textual references.
AO5	Communicate clearly, effectively and imaginatively, selecting and adapting tone, style and register for different forms, purposes and audiences. Organise information and ideas, using structural and grammatical features to support coherence and cohesion of texts.
AO6	Use a range of vocabulary and sentence structures for clarity, purpose and effect, with accurate spelling and punctuation.

How this workbook is structured

The workbook is divided into four chapters. The chapters are self-contained so they can be used in any order.

• Chapter 1 and Chapter 2 focus on Paper 1. Each chapter consists of a complete stand-alone exam paper: source texts, question paper and mark scheme. The source texts reflect the type of text you will be reading and responding to in your exam and the questions are also typical of what you will encounter. There are then follow-up sections with advice and activities so that you can improve the quality of your initial responses after you have attempted each practice Paper 1 exam paper.

• Chapter 3 and Chapter 4 focus on Paper 2. Again, each chapter consists of a complete stand-alone exam paper: source texts, question paper and mark scheme. The source texts reflect the type of texts you will be reading and responding to in your exam and the questions are also typical of what you will encounter. Again, there are then follow-up sections with advice and activities so that you can improve the quality of your initial responses after you have attempted each practice Paper 2 exam paper.

What are the main features within this workbook?

Preparing to practice

Before you attempt each practice exam paper, you are reminded of which skills are being assessed in each question and what you are expected to do to demonstrate those skills.

Unpicking the mark scheme

Before you attempt each practice exam paper, the mark scheme is unpicked to show how levels and marks are awarded by the examiner. Key words are explained and skill strands in the Indicative Standard are highlighted. This can help you to improve the quality of your work because you will understand exactly what is expected of you in each question.

Tips

There are also some tips on how best to approach each question.

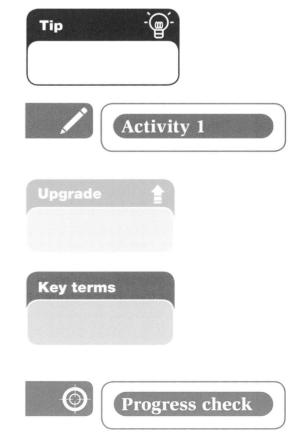

Activities

After you have attempted the practice exam paper, you will find activities to help you improve your initial responses for each question.

Upgrade

You will also find tips to help you move up the mark scheme and focus on specific areas to improve.

Key terms

This feature helps support your understanding of key terms. For ease of reference, there is also a complete list of key terms at the end of the workbook.

Progress check

At the end of each chapter you will find Progress checks. These enable you to use self-assessment to establish how confident you feel about what you have been learning and help you to identify areas for further practice.

Chapter 1: Sample exam paper 1

Source A: 21st-century prose-fiction

This is an extract from the beginning of a novel, The Child's Elephant *by Rachel Campbell-Johnson, published in 2013. A seven-year-old boy named Bat is herding cattle in the wide, open grasslands of the African savannah when the peaceful atmosphere is suddenly shattered.*

The sound of a rifle shot rang through the air. For a few moments it seemed as if the whole   1
world had stopped. The **cicadas** fell silent, a bush rat dived for its burrow, the cattle paused
in their chewing and looked upwards with wide empty stares; and Bat, the lone herd-boy who
up till then had been dreaming, swishing at bushes with a long whippy branch, let the switch
fall and dropped suddenly down on his haunches. His head was quite hidden by the tall,   5
yellow grass.   6

He felt the slow, rolling shudder through the soles of his feet. It rumbled his bones like the beat   7
of the big tribal drum. Something that mattered had just happened out there on the savannah.
He could feel it: something momentous that he didn't want to know about and yet knew at the
same time he would have to find out. But not now, he thought, as he ducked even lower in   10
the grasses. He let his breath leak through fingers clamped hard to his mouth. A lizard clung
spellbound to a stalk right beside him. He gazed into the rapt gold-ringed bead of its eye. It
stared back, unblinking, as if it had been stunned.   13

He listened. Somewhere not so very far away he could hear people talking. The sound drifted
like wood-smoke upon a slack wind: murmuring voices . . . then a clatter of laughter . . . the   15
silence that followed it . . . then a sudden angry shout . . . then nothing again.

Who was it? He could feel his pulse racing. His heart jumped in his throat. Every shift of the
breeze could have been someone approaching; every glint of the light could have been a
stranger's glance. Was someone even now stealing up on him? Unable to bear the uncertainty,
he rose to his feet.   20

Nothing looked very different. The cattle were peaceful; a new calf was suckling; the scrublands   21
that stretched all about him looked quite undisturbed. It was funny how hiding played tricks
with your imagination. He shouldn't have allowed himself to get so scared, he thought. He was
seven after all: far too old to be behaving like some panicky chicken.

Ducking his head low, Bat set off through the grasses. Their tall, feathered fronds brushed as   25
high as his chest. His eyes darted warily as he slipped through the thorn bushes.

After a while, he began to see traces; he started noticing places where the scrub had been
squashed. Branches were broken and bushes were flattened. He slowed up his pace as he
crested a ridge. The down-slope was stony. He would have to be careful not to trip. Flitting
between boulders, half running, half scrambling, he arrived at a river-bed that had all but run   30
dry. It was then that he spotted the footprint which brought him suddenly up short. It was huge!
His heart thumped. It was truly gigantic, he thought, as big as the biggest circle that he could
have made if, stretching out both arms as wide as he was able, he had then brought them
round and tried to brush fingertips.

Bat swallowed. He'd already come too far . . . far further than he'd first meant to . . . much   35
further than anyone would have told him was safe. He cast a quick backwards glance. He could

no longer see his cattle. The dry riverbed glittered and flashed in the heat. On the far bank was a thicket. Something had crashed straight through it. A bush was splattered with red. Perhaps it was a flower, the boy found himself hoping; but he didn't need to look a second time to know that it was not: it was blood. 40

He scuttled for the cover of some rocks ahead. Beyond, he could now see a vast shadowy shape. From where he was crouching, it loomed high as a mountain. It blocked out the horizon. It blocked out, for a moment, all the thoughts in his head. But then, with a jolt, the full truth broke upon him. This mountainous form was a dead elephant.

Glossary: **cicadas:** small winged insects which make a clicking song-like noise

Section A: Reading

Answer **all** questions in this section.

You are advised to spend about 45 minutes on this section.

01 Read again the first part of the source, from **lines 1 to 6.**

List **four** things that happen after the rifle shot from this part of the source.

[4 marks]

02 Look in detail at this extract, from **lines 7 to 13** of the source.

He felt the slow, rolling shudder through the soles of his feet. It rumbled his bones like the beat of the big tribal drum. Something that mattered had just happened out there on the savannah. He could feel it: something momentous that he didn't want to know about and yet knew at the same time he would have to find out. But not now, he thought, as he ducked even lower in the grasses. He let his breath leak through fingers clamped hard to his mouth. A lizard clung spellbound to a stalk right beside him. He gazed into the rapt gold-ringed bead of its eye. It stared back, unblinking, as if it had been stunned.

How does the writer use language here to describe the reaction to what is happening nearby?

You could include the writer's choice of:

- words and phrases
- language features and techniques
- sentence forms.

[8 marks]

03 You now need to think about the **whole** of the source.

This text is the opening of a novel.

How has the writer structured the text to interest you as a reader?

You could write about:

- what the writer focuses your attention on at the beginning of the source
- how and why the writer changes this focus as the source develops
- any other structural features that interest you.

[8 marks]

0 4 Focus this part of your answer on the second part of the source, from **line 21 to the end**.

A student said, 'This part of the story, where Bat investigates what has happened, shows that he's struggling to accept that it's something bad, even though it's obvious.'

To what extent do you agree?

In your response, you could:

- consider your own impressions of Bat
- evaluate how the writer shows that something bad has happened
- support your response with references to the text.

[20 marks]

Section B: Writing

You are advised to spend about 45 minutes on this section.

Write in full sentences.

You are reminded of the need to plan your answer.

You should leave enough time to check your work at the end.

0 5 Your local newspaper is running a creative writing competition and they intend to publish the best entries.

Either

Write a story about an encounter with animals as suggested by this picture:

or

Describe a journey that leads to a discovery.

(24 marks for content and organisation
16 marks for technical accuracy)

[40 marks]

Preparing to practise

Before you attempt this practice exam paper, it is important to remember which skills are being assessed in each question and what you are expected to do to demonstrate those skills. Read through the following and think about the Tips for each question.

Question 1

Example Exam Question

01 Read again the first part of the source, from **lines 1 to 6**.

List **four** things that happen after the rifle shot from this part of the source.

[4 marks]

You should spend about 3 minutes on this question.

Skills and objectives

• To identify and interpret explicit and implicit information **(AO1)**

What you have to do

• Find four things in the given lines about the given focus. In this practice exam paper you have to find **four** things that **happen after the rifle shot** in **lines 1 to 6**.

Tips

• Make sure you select points from the correct lines.

• Select at least four points.

• Start each point with the focus of the question, e.g. 'After the rifle shot...' so that the points you make are relevant.

• Retrieve points rather than trying to interpret the source – in case you actually misinterpret the text!

Question 2

Example Exam Question

02 Look in detail at **lines 7 to 13** of the source.

How does the writer use language here to describe the reaction to what is happening nearby?

You could include the writer's choice of:

- words and phrases
- language features and techniques
- sentence forms.

[8 marks]

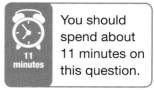 You should spend about 11 minutes on this question.

Skills and objectives

- To analyse how the writer's use of language achieves effects **(AO2)**

What you have to do

- Choose some examples of language. In this practice exam paper you have to focus on language **in lines 7 to 13** used **to describe the reaction to what is happening nearby**.

- Write about the effects of your selected examples of language.

- Use subject terminology to enhance your response.

Tips

- Make sure you select examples of language from the correct lines.

- Remember that the most important part of this question is the **quality** of what you write about the **effects of language**. Your comments have to be **precise** and **contextualised** in order to achieve Level 3 and above.

- Notice the word 'could' in the question. You 'could' write about words and phrases, language features and techniques or sentence forms, but you don't have to write about all of them.

- Zoom in on individual words and phrases to analyse their effects.

Key term

contextualise: to analyse a word or phrase in terms of the words or ideas surrounding it

Question 3

Example Exam Question

03 You now need to think about the **whole** of the source.

This text is the opening of a novel.

How has the writer structured the text to interest you as a reader?

You could write about:

* what the writer focuses your attention on at the beginning of the source

* how and why the writer changes this focus as the source develops

* any other structural features that interest you.

[8 marks]

 You should spend about 11 minutes on this question.

Skills and objectives

* To analyse how the writer's use of **structure** achieves effects **(AO2)**

What you have to do

* Choose some examples of structural features from the **whole** source.

* Write about the effects of your selected examples of structure.

* Use subject terminology to enhance your response.

Key term

structure: the organisation of the text, how it is introduced, presented and concluded; structure also includes how paragraphs and ideas are grouped or linked together

Tips

* Make sure you select examples of structure from the **whole** source.

* Remember that the most important part of this question is the **quality** of what you write about the **effects of structural features**. Your comments have to be **precise** and **contextualised** in order to achieve Level 3 and above.

* Consider 'Where? What? Why?' and ask yourself the question: 'How does reading about this **at this point** add to my understanding of the whole source?'

* Look at the sequencing, structural shifts and movement through the text, and write about the possible reasons behind these structural choices. Try to make links and connections between different parts of the text.

Question 4

Example Exam Question

04 Focus this part of your answer on the second part of the source, from **line 21 to the end**.

A student said, 'This part of story, where Bat investigates what has happened, shows that he's struggling to accept that it's something bad, even though it's obvious.'

To what extent do you agree?

In your response, you could:

- consider your own impressions of Bat
- evaluate how the writer shows that something bad has happened
- support your response with references to the text.

[20 marks]

You should spend about 20 minutes on this question.

Skills and objectives

- To evaluate the text critically and support this with appropriate textual references **(AO4)**

What you have to do

- Evaluate the ideas in the text. In this practice exam paper you are directed to the second part of the source **from line 21**. You have to consider **your own impressions of Bat** and also **how the writer shows that something bad has happened**.

- Evaluate the effects of the writer's methods used to convey these ideas.

- Support your evaluation with textual references.

- Focus on the given statement. In this practice exam paper, the focus is on **Bat's struggle to accept something bad has happened.**

Tips

- Make sure you focus your evaluation on the correct lines.

- Think of evaluation as the **interpretation** of content (the 'what') and **analysis** of method ('the how') in relation to a given statement.

- Make sure you evaluate the 'how' as well as the 'what'.

- Remember that the most important part of this question is the **quality** of what you write about **both the ideas and the writer's methods used to convey these ideas**. Your comments have to be **precise** and **contextualised** in order to achieve Level 3 and above.

- There are no right or wrong answers – before you start to write, separate the different elements of the question, decide if you agree, partially agree or disagree, and then select relevant evidence from the text to support your opinions.

Question 5

Example Exam Question

05 Your local newspaper is running a creative writing competition and they intend to publish the best entries.

Either Write a story about an encounter with animals as suggested by the picture.

or Describe a journey that leads to a discovery.

[40 marks]

You should spend about 35 minutes on this question: 5 minutes to plan, 25 minutes to write and 5 minutes to check at the end.

Skills and objectives

- To communicate effectively and imaginatively in an appropriate style according to purpose and audience **(AO5)**
- To organise information and ideas, using structural and grammatical features **(AO5)**
- To write clearly and accurately **(AO6)**

What you have to do

- Produce a piece of imaginative writing that communicates to the reader.
- Demonstrate the ability to match **tone**, style and register to purpose and audience.
- Use effective vocabulary and phrasing.
- Use effective **linguistic devices**.
- Structure your writing effectively.
- Engage the reader through your choice of subject matter and use of detail.
- Link and develop your ideas.
- Use paragraphs and **discourse markers** effectively.
- Write accurately.

Tips

- Remember that what is being assessed is the **quality** of your writing. You have to communicate **clearly** in order to reach Level 3 or above.
- Take time to plan your response before you start writing, e.g. if you chose the narrative option, think about plot, setting, characterisation, viewpoint, structure and atmosphere.
- Adopt a quality rather than quantity approach – a shorter, crafted response is better than a longer, rambling one.
- Leave time at the end to proofread your response, and correct and improve where possible.

Activity 1: Answering the practice exam paper

Using all the tips you have read above, complete the practice exam paper on pages 6–9.

Key terms

discourse marker: a word or phrase that helps to manage and organise the flow and structure of writing, e.g. *but*, *although* etc.

linguistic devices: words or phrases that convey meaning which is different to the literal meaning of the words. Those most useful in imaginative writing include:

- **metaphor:** a comparison showing the similarity between two quite different things, stating that one actually *is* the other

- **simile:** a comparison showing the similarity between two quite different things, stating that one is like the other

tone: manner of expression that shows the writer's attitude, e.g. humorous or sarcastic

Unpicking the mark scheme

A mark scheme is used to assess the quality of your response for each question. Unpicking the mark scheme can show you how the levels and marks are awarded. This can help you to improve the quality of your work because you will understand exactly what is expected of you in each question.

Question 1 mark scheme

Example Exam Question

01 List **four** things that happen after the rifle shot from **lines 1 to 6** of the source.

[4 marks]

Question 1 is different from all the other Reading questions because it is the only question where the answers are either right or wrong. You are awarded 1 mark for each correct point, up to a total of 4 marks.

What follows is the Question 1 mark scheme for the practice exam paper on pages 6–9.

Indicative content; students may include:
- After the rifle shot, it was like the whole world stopped
- The cicadas fell silent
- A bush rat dived for its burrow
- The cattle stopped chewing
- The cattle looked upwards
- Bat let go of his switch
- Bat dropped down on his haunches
- Bat hid in the grass

Or any other valid responses that you are able to verify by checking the source.

These are not the only correct answers. The mark scheme includes the instruction 'Or any other valid responses that you are able to verify by checking the source' because there may be other correct points that are not listed here, e.g. 'Bat stopped dreaming' would also be awarded 1 mark.

Other mark scheme instructions for Question 1 can also help you to be clear about how to answer this question:

- You can only be awarded a mark if you select from the correct lines and what you select is correct.

- You can only be awarded a mark if what you select is relevant, i.e. something that happens after the rifle shot.

- You can use the exact words from the text or you can use your own words.

- If you include more than one point in a line, you will be awarded a mark for each point, as long as the point is relevant.

- If you copy out the whole section word for word, you will not be awarded any marks because you have not demonstrated the ability to select relevant points.

Improving your Question 1 response

Activity 2: Self-assessment

a. Look again at your original response to Question 1. Decide how many marks you would be awarded at the moment. Use the mark scheme on page 15 to help you make your decision.

b. Reread lines 1 to 6. Using the mark scheme as a guide, circle each individual point showing what happens after the rifle shot as you read.

c. Choose which additional points you will add to your response and write them out.

d. Look at your whole response and see if you have now achieved a higher mark.

Tip

In a question where you need to find particular details, circling points as you read can be helpful when you then come to write your answer out.

Question 2 mark scheme

Example Exam Question

02 How does the writer use language in **lines 7 to 13** to describe the reaction to what is happening nearby?

You could include the writer's choice of:

• words and phrases

• language features and techniques

• sentence forms.

[8 marks]

The mark scheme for Question 2 consists of three columns:

• **Level:** There are four levels, with Level 1 at the bottom to Level 4 at the top. Each level has key words that sum up the quality of responses in that level.

Level	Key words	Explanation
Level 4	'Detailed' and 'perceptive'	This means you are seeing meaning deep below the surface and your analysis of the writer's use of language is insightful and astute.
Level 3	'Clear' and 'Relevant'	This means your explanation of the writer's use of language is developed, precise and contextualised.
Level 2	'Some understanding and comment'	This means you are trying to comment on the writer's use of language and having some success, but what you're saying is undeveloped and not yet clear.
Level 1	'Simple' and 'Limited'	This means what you are saying about the writer's use of language is basic and obvious.

- **Skills descriptors:** This column shows the skills being assessed in Question 2. Your response is placed in a level according to how well you have demonstrated the key skill – writing about the effects of the writer's choice of language. How well you demonstrate the other skills determines your mark within that level.

- **Indicative standard:** This column shows the **quality** of response that is expected at each level. It does not show the correct answer in terms of content because you may not select the same examples of language, but the quality of your analysis of language will be matched against the quality of these comments.

What follows is the Question 2 mark scheme for the practice exam paper on pages 6–9. Because the most important part of this question is the **quality** of what you write about the effects of language, this key skill has been highlighted so that you can trace the thread through the mark scheme levels to see the progression from Level 1 to Level 4.

> **Key term**
>
> **judicious:** showing considered judgement

Level	Skills descriptors	Indicative standard
Level 4 Detailed, perceptive analysis 7–8 marks	Shows detailed and perceptive understanding of language: • Analyses the effects of the writer's choices of language • Selects a range of **judicious** textual detail • Makes sophisticated and accurate use of subject terminology	The writer uses an apt simile with connotations of Africa to describe Bat's reaction to what is happening nearby: a shudder 'rumbled his bones like the beat of the big tribal drum'. This suggests his fear of these unknown events that are obviously significant is so overwhelming that it physically manifests itself in the very core of his being. It is like uncontrollable thunder reverberating deep in his soul. The wildlife reacts in a similar way, because a lizard 'clung spellbound to a stalk right beside him' and behaves as if 'rapt' and 'stunned'. This extended metaphor of startled fascination implies the creature is transfixed, almost hypnotised, into a fear-induced paralysis.
Level 3 Clear, relevant explanation 5–6 marks	Shows clear understanding of language: • Explains clearly the effects of the writer's choices of language • Selects a range of relevant textual detail • Makes clear and accurate use of subject terminology	Bat's reaction to what is happening nearby is a shudder that 'rumbled his bones like the beat of the big tribal drum'. This simile suggests Bat is so scared he feels as if a repeated thumping is rolling through his body, similar to the pulse of African drumming that would be familiar to him. A lizard also reacts in a fearful way, and 'clung spellbound to a stalk right beside him'. The word 'spellbound' implies the lizard is riveted to the spot, its attention so fixed on what is happening nearby that it's dazed and unable to move.

Level	Skills descriptors	Indicative standard
Level 2 Some understanding and comment 3–4 marks	Shows some understanding of language: • Attempts to comment on the effect of language • Selects some appropriate textual detail • Makes some use of subject terminology, mainly appropriately	The writer says a shudder 'rumbled his bones like the beat of the big tribal drum'. This simile shows that Bat is scared of what is happening nearby and his body reacts as if something is hitting him. There's also a lizard that 'clung spellbound to a stalk right beside him', so the lizard reacts scared as well. 'Spellbound' makes it sound as if it's aware of what's going on, but not in a good way.
Level 1 Simple, limited comment 1–2 marks	Shows simple awareness of language: • Offers simple comment on the effect of language • Selects simple reference(s) or textual detail(s) • Makes simple use of subject terminology, not always appropriately	Bat has a shudder that 'rumbled his bones', so it's saying there's a rumble going through his body. A lizard 'clung spellbound to a stalk right beside him', which means the lizard doesn't like what's happening.

Activity 3: Tracking levels of response

a. To help you see the progression more clearly, choose one comment in the highlighted Level 1 indicative standard response, e.g. 'which means the lizard doesn't like what's happening'. Copy it out, and then write down the improved version of this comment shown at Level 2, Level 3 and Level 4. Look at the quality of the comment demonstrated in each level.

b. Think about how you could improve your own response.

Improving your Question 2 response

Activity 4: Self-assessment

a. Look again at your original response to Question 2. Decide which level your response fits into at the moment. Use the mark scheme on pages 17–18 to help you make your decision.

b. Think about which parts of your response you could develop in order to improve it. Look in particular at the **quality** of what you have written about the effects of language.

- Look at the difference in the skills descriptor bullets at different levels. For example, a response needs to develop from 'attempts to comment' into 'explains clearly' in order to move from Level 2 to Level 3.
- Work in steps: What word/phrase/language feature have you selected? How has the writer used it to create an effect? Why might the writer have intended this effect?
- The better you link these elements together, the more successful your response should be.

c. Consider the Upgrade advice in the panel.

d. Rewrite your response with the parts you have developed, and see if you have now achieved a higher mark.

Upgrade

- Think about the effect of the writer's choice of individual words, e.g. 'he let his breath leak through fingers clamped hard to his mouth'. Why are the words 'leak' and 'clamped' particularly successful?
- When discussing the effects of language, remember it is important to consider the context in which the words and phrases are used, and to be precise when commenting on effect.
- Using a phrase such as 'This suggests...' shows that you are beginning to interpret the effect of the writer's language used to describe the reaction to what is happening nearby. Other useful phrases include: 'This means...', 'This lets us know...', 'This indicates...', 'This implies...' and 'This makes me think...'.

Question 3 mark scheme

Example Exam Question

03 This text is the opening of a novel.

How has the writer structured the text to interest you as a reader?

You could write about:

- what the writer focuses your attention on at the beginning of the source

- how and why the writer changes this focus as the source develops

- any other structural features that interest you.

[8 marks]

The mark scheme for Question 3 consists of three columns:

- **Level:** There are four levels, with Level 1 at the bottom to Level 4 at the top. Each level has key words that sum up the quality of responses in that level.

Level	Key words	Explanation
Level 4	'Detailed' and 'perceptive'	This means you are seeing meaning deep below the surface and your analysis of the writer's use of structure is insightful and astute.
Level 3	'Clear' and 'relevant'	This means your explanation of the writer's use of structure is developed, precise and contextualised.
Level 2	'Some understanding and comment'	This means you are trying to comment on the writer's use of structure and having some success, but what you're saying is undeveloped and not yet clear.
Level 1	'Simple' and 'Limited'	This means what you are saying about the writer's use of structure is basic and obvious.

- **Skills descriptors:** This column shows the skills being assessed in Question 3. Your response is placed in a level according to how well you have demonstrated the key skill – writing about the effects of the writer's choice of structural features. How well you demonstrate the other skills determines your mark within that level.

- **Indicative standard:** This column shows the **quality** of response that is expected at each level. It does not show the correct answer in terms of content because you may not select the same examples of structure, but the quality of your analysis of structure will be matched against the quality of these indicative standard responses.

What follows is the Question 3 mark scheme for the practice exam paper on pages 6–9. Because the most important part of this question is the **quality** of what you write about the effects of structural features, this key skill has been highlighted so that you can trace the thread through the mark scheme levels to see the progression from Level 1 to Level 4.

Level	Skills descriptors	Indicative standard
Level 4 Detailed, perceptive analysis 7–8 marks	Shows detailed and perceptive understanding of structural features: • Analyses the effects of the writer's choices of structural features • Selects a range of judicious examples • Makes sophisticated and accurate use of subject terminology	The text has an interesting circular structure in that a mystery is established in the opening line and solved in the concluding sentence. The writer begins mid-action by zooming in on 'the sound of a rifle shot' in the open grasslands of Africa. This first sentence creates an urgent, abrupt opening with a sense of immediacy, and generates an atmosphere of intrigue as to the victim. The focus then switches to Bat, who believes 'something that mattered had just happened out there on the savannah' and it's 'something momentous'. The rifle shot is obviously significant, although the repetition of 'something' emphasises we still don't know the specific target. The reader then goes on Bat's journey with him as he discovers clues that are increasingly disturbing, including a 'gigantic' footprint and a thicket that 'something had crashed straight through'. When Bat finds the body of the 'dead elephant' in the final paragraph, this resolution provides the reader with the answer as to what was killed by the gun in the opening line, and the mystery is solved.
Level 3 Clear, relevant explanation 5–6 marks	Shows clear understanding of structural features: • Explains clearly the effects of the writer's choices of structural features • Selects a range of relevant examples • Makes clear and accurate use of subject terminology	At the beginning the writer zooms in on 'the sound of a rifle shot' and the reader immediately feels worried due to being plunged into the middle of a dramatic and potentially dangerous scene. The focus then switches to Bat, who thinks 'something that mattered had just happened' and that it's 'something momentous'. His thoughts are important at this point because they confirm our earlier worries that the rifle shot meant drama and danger. The text then follows a chronological structure through the sights Bat witnesses, such as a 'gigantic' footprint and a thicket that 'something had crashed straight through'. In the final paragraph, Bat discovers the body of a dead elephant, and this fills in the missing piece of the puzzle as we now learn what was killed by the gun in the opening line.
Level 2 Some understanding and comment 3–4 marks	Shows some understanding of structural features: • Attempts to comment on the effect of structural features • Selects some appropriate examples • Makes some use of subject terminology, mainly appropriately	At the beginning, we learn that 'the sound of a rifle shot rang through the air', so straight away we know the story is going to be dramatic and probably bad. Then the focus shifts to Bat, who thinks 'something that mattered had just happened'. He then sees things like a 'gigantic' footprint and at the end he finds a dead elephant, which could be the bad thing.

Level	Skills descriptors	Indicative standard
Level 1 Simple, limited comment 1–2 marks	Shows simple awareness of structural features: • Offers simple comment on the effect of structure • Selects simple reference(s) or example(s) • Makes simple use of subject terminology, not always appropriately	At the beginning the focus is on 'the sound of a rifle shot', and this makes us think someone could have been murdered. Then later Bat finds a big footprint and then a dead elephant, so it's an animal, not a person that's dead.

Activity 5: Tracking levels of response

a. To help you see the progression more clearly, choose one comment in the highlighted Level 1 indicative standard response, e.g. 'so it's an animal, not a person that's dead'. Copy it out, and then write down the improved version of this comment shown at Level 2, Level 3, and Level 4. Look at the quality of comment demonstrated in each level.

b. Think about how you could improve your own response.

Improving your Question 3 response

Activity 6: Self-assessment

a. Look again at your original response to Question 3. Decide which level your response fits into at the moment. Use the mark scheme on pages 21–22 to help you make your decision.

b. Think about which parts of your response you could develop in order to improve it. Look in particular at the **quality** of what you have written about the effects of structural features.

   • Look at the difference in the skills descriptor bullets between Levels. For example, a response needs to develop from 'attempts to comment' into 'explains clearly' in order to move from Level 2 to Level 3.
   • Work in steps. Consider 'Where? What? Why?' and ask yourself the question 'How does reading about this **at this point** add to my understanding of the whole source?'
   • The better you link these elements together, the more successful your answer should be.

c. Consider the Upgrade advice in the panel.

d. Rewrite your response with the parts you have developed, and see if you have now achieved a higher mark.

Upgrade

- Remember to look at the sequencing, structural shifts and movement through the text, and write about the possible reasons behind these structural choices.
- Structural shifts that are relevant to this text include:
  - zooming in from something big to something much smaller
  - shifting between different places
  - the introduction of new characters at a significant point
  - combining external actions with internal thoughts
  - developing and reiterating, i.e. focusing on an important idea and repeating it
  - circular structure – returning at the end to what happened at the beginning
  - positioning of key sentences and their impact on the whole
- Remember to make links and connections between these different parts of the text.

Question 4 mark scheme

Example Exam Question

04 A student said, 'This part of the story (line 21 to the end), where Bat investigates what has happened, shows that he's struggling to accept that it's something bad, even though it's obvious.'

To what extent do you agree?

In your response, you could:

- consider your own impressions of Bat
- evaluate how the writer shows that something bad has happened
- support your response with references to the text.

[20 marks]

The mark scheme for Question 4 consists of three columns:

- **Level:** There are four levels, with Level 1 at the bottom to Level 4 at the top. Each level has key words that sum up the quality of responses in that level.

Level	Key words	Explanation
Level 4	'Detailed' and 'perceptive'	This means you are seeing meaning deep below the surface and your evaluation of ideas and/or the writer's methods is insightful and astute.
Level 3	'Clear' and 'Relevant'	This means your evaluation of ideas and/or the writer's methods is developed, precise and contextualised.
Level 2	'Some evaluation'	This means you are trying to evaluate ideas and/or the writer's methods and having some success, but what you're saying is undeveloped and not yet clear.
Level 1	'Simple' and 'Limited'	This means your evaluation of ideas and/or the writer's methods is basic and obvious.

- **Skills descriptors:** This column shows the skills being assessed in Question 4. Your response is placed in a level according to how well you have demonstrated the key skills – writing about the ideas and the writer's methods used to convey these ideas. How well you demonstrate the other skills determines your mark within that level.

- **Indicative standard:** This column shows the **quality** of response that is expected at each level. It does not show the correct answer in terms of content because you may not evaluate the same ideas or the same writer's methods, but the quality of your evaluation will be matched against the quality of these comments.

What follows is the Question 4 mark scheme for the practice exam paper on pages 6–9. Because the most important part of this question is the **quality** of your evaluation of ideas and the writer's methods used to convey these ideas, these key skills have been highlighted so that you can trace the threads through the mark scheme levels to see the progression from Level 1 to Level 4. Green highlighting shows comments evaluating the relevant ideas; yellow highlighting shows comments on the writer's methods.

Level	Skills descriptors	Indicative standard
Level 4 Detailed, perceptive evaluation 16–20 marks	Shows detailed and perceptive evaluation: • Evaluates critically and in detail the effect(s) on the reader • Shows perceptive understanding of writer's methods • Selects a range of judicious textual detail • Develops a convincing and critical response to the focus of the statement	For most of this extract Bat is in denial. When he comes out of hiding, he thinks 'nothing looked very different', but despite the 'peaceful' cattle and 'undisturbed' scrublands, I think he knows there is trouble ahead and subconsciously he's lying to himself. He's definitely struggling because calling himself a 'panicky chicken' is his child-like way of lightening the mood in order to convince himself that he's being irrational. There are many 'traces' that something bad has happened, but I think he chooses to ignore them because it's safer to pretend there's a logical explanation and that way he can postpone the inevitable. Even when he sees a bush 'splattered with red', he 'found himself hoping' it was just a flower rather than blood. However, the passive verb 'found himself' suggests he's almost hoping against his will, and definitely against his better judgement in the face of such overwhelming evidence. When he eventually comes across a 'vast shadowy shape', his struggle is over as he is forced to accept the horror of what has been inevitable all along: an elephant has been killed. The full truth 'broke upon him', implying this sudden realisation has erupted violently within him and any remaining hope has been destroyed.

Level	Skills descriptors	Indicative standard
Level 3 Clear, relevant evaluation 11–15 marks	Shows clear and relevant evaluation: • Evaluates clearly the effect(s) on the reader • Shows clear understanding of writer's methods • Selects a range of relevant textual references • Makes a clear and relevant response to the focus of the statement	When Bat comes out of hiding, he calls himself a 'panicky chicken' in an attempt to convince himself that he has over-reacted to the situation. However, there are many 'traces' that something bad has happened, including a bush 'splattered with red', and I agree Bat is struggling because he seems to ignore all the evidence. He is even 'hoping' this red is just a flower, but the verb 'hoping' implies that although he desperately wants it to be just a flower, deep down he knows that it's blood. When he eventually sees a 'vast shadowy shape' his struggle is over and he is forced to accept the truth that an elephant has been killed. This realisation 'broke upon him', suggesting that reality has burst inside him and he can't argue with it any longer.
Level 2 Some evaluation 6–10 marks	Shows some attempts at evaluation: • Makes some evaluative comment(s) on effect(s) on the reader • Shows some understanding of writer's methods • Selects some appropriate textual reference(s) • Makes some response to the focus of the statement	I agree. Bat doesn't want to believe that something bad has happened. He calls himself a 'panicky chicken' because he thinks he's just being silly. He starts to change his mind a bit when he sees lots of signs that things aren't right, but even then he pretends that the red 'splattered' on a bush is a flower. It says he's 'hoping' so he really wants it to be just a flower and nothing worse. At the end he has to accept something bad has happened because he finds a dead elephant. It says the truth 'broke upon him', so it's like his hopes of everything being ok are smashed.
Level 1 Simple, limited comment 1–5 marks	Shows simple, limited evaluation: • Makes simple, limited evaluative comment(s) on effect(s) on reader • Shows limited understanding of writer's methods • Selects simple, limited textual reference(s) • Makes a simple, limited response to the focus of the statement	Bat says he's just a 'panicky chicken' but I agree he's struggling. It's obvious that something bad has happened because there's a bush that's 'splattered with red'. Bat is 'hoping' it's a flower because that's what he wants it to be. He finds a dead elephant at the end so he can't pretend any more. The truth 'broke upon him' like it hit him in the face.

Activity 7: Tracking levels of response

a. To help you see the progression more clearly, choose one comment in the highlighted Level 1 indicative standard response, e.g. 'The truth "broke upon him" like it hit him in the face'. Copy it out, and then write down the improved version of this comment shown at Level 2, Level 3, and Level 4. Look at the quality of comment demonstrated in each level.

b. Think about how you could improve your own response.

Improving your Question 4 response

Activity 8: Self-assessment

a. Look again at your original response to Question 4. Decide which level your response fits into at the moment. Use the mark scheme on pages 24–25 to help you make your decision.

b. Think about which parts of your response you could develop in order to improve it. Look in particular at the **quality** of your evaluation of ideas and the writer's methods used to convey these ideas.

- Look at the difference in the skills descriptor bullets at different levels. For example, a response needs to develop from 'shows some understanding' into 'shows clear understanding' in order to move from Level 2 to Level 3.
- Work in steps. What relevant ideas have you identified to evaluate? What methods has the writer used to convey those ideas?
- The better you link these elements together, the more successful your answer should be.

c. Consider the Upgrade advice in the panel.

d. Rewrite your response with the parts you have developed, and see if you have now achieved a higher mark.

Upgrade

- Look for evidence that something bad has happened, plus evidence that Bat is struggling to accept it and also evidence that he has to accept it. Then decide whether or not you agree, partially agree or disagree, with the given statement.
- As part of your evaluation, remember you are expected to interpret, as well as identify, the relevant ideas.
- Make sure you also evaluate the effects of the writer's methods used to convey the ideas. In this text you could consider not only language and structure but also **narrative voice**.

Key term

narrative voice: the characteristic ways in which the narrator speaks and thinks

Question 5 mark scheme

Example Exam Question

05 Write a story about an encounter with animals as suggested by the picture.

or

Describe a journey that leads to a discovery.

[40 marks]

In Question 5 you will be assessed on:

- Content and Organisation **(AO5)**
- Technical Accuracy **(AO6)**.

So the mark scheme for Question 5 is divided into two parts.

The mark scheme for Content and Organisation (AO5) consists of three columns:

- **Level:** There are four levels, with Level 1 at the bottom to Level 4 at the top. Each level has key words that sum up the quality of responses in that level.

Level	Key words	Explanation
Level 4	'Compelling, convincing communication'	This means that your writing is crafted for impact. Ideas are linked in a confident, seamless manner and form a unified whole. Your reader is gripped and emotionally involved in the outcome.
Level 3	'Consistent, clear communication'	This means that your writing is shaped, fluent and makes sense as a whole. Ideas are effectively linked, developed and relevant to purpose. Your reader is interested in finding out what happens.
Level 2	'Some successful communication'	This means that your writing makes sense at times. Some ideas are linked but others may be illogical or undeveloped. Your reader is interested in parts but loses the thread of what you're saying.
Level 1	'Simple, limited communication'	This means that your writing doesn't always make sense. Ideas are basic and may be rambling and not well organised. Your reader struggles to follow what you are saying.

- **Sub-level:** Each of the four levels is broken down into an upper level and a lower level. To move into an upper level you have to demonstrate a higher level of skill or sustain the skills in the lower half of the level.

- **Skills descriptors:** This column shows the skills being assessed in Question 5. Your response is placed in a level according to how well you have demonstrated the key skill – overall communication. How well you demonstrate the other skills determines your mark within that level.

What follows is the Question 5 Mark Scheme for Content and Organisation (AO5) for the practice exam paper on pages 6–9. Because the most important part of this question is the **quality** of your overall communication, this key skill has been highlighted so that you can trace the thread through the mark scheme levels to see the progression from Level 1 to Level 4.

Level	Sub-level	Skills descriptors
Level 4 Compelling, convincing communication 19–24 marks	Upper Level 4 22–24 marks	**Content** • Communication is convincing and compelling • Tone, style and register are assuredly matched to purpose and audience • Extensive and ambitious vocabulary with sustained crafting of linguistic devices **Organisation** • Varied and inventive use of structural features • Writing is compelling, incorporating a range of convincing and complex ideas • Fluently linked paragraphs with seamlessly integrated discourse markers
	Lower Level 4 19–21 marks	**Content** • Communication is convincing • Tone, style and register are convincingly matched to purpose and audience • Extensive vocabulary with conscious crafting of linguistic devices **Organisation** • Varied and effective structural features • Writing is highly engaging with a range of developed complex ideas • Consistently coherent use of paragraphs with integrated discourse markers
Level 3 Consistent, clear communication 13–18 marks	Upper Level 3 16–18 marks	**Content** • Communication is consistently clear • Tone, style and register are clearly and consistently matched to purpose and audience • Increasingly sophisticated vocabulary and phrasing, chosen for effect with a range of successful linguistic devices **Organisation** • Effective use of structural features • Writing is engaging, using a range of clear connected ideas • Coherent paragraphs with integrated discourse markers

Level	Sub-level	Skills descriptors
	Lower Level 3 13–15 marks	**Content** • Communication is generally clear • Tone, style and register are generally matched to purpose and audience • Vocabulary clearly chosen for effect and appropriate use of linguistic devices **Organisation** • Usually effective use of structural features • Writing is engaging, with a range of connected ideas • Usually coherent paragraphs with range of discourse markers
Level 2 Some successful communication 7–12 marks	Upper Level 2 10–12 marks	**Content** • Communicates with some sustained success • Some sustained attempt to match tone, style and register to purpose and audience • Conscious use of vocabulary with some use of linguistic devices **Organisation** • Some use of structural features • Increasing variety of linked and relevant ideas • Some use of paragraphs and some use of discourse markers
	Lower Level 2 7–9 marks	**Content** • Communicates with some success • Attempts to match tone, style and register to purpose and audience • Begins to vary vocabulary with some use of linguistic devices **Organisation** • Attempts to use structural features • Some linked and relevant ideas • Attempts to write in paragraphs with some discourse markers, not always appropriate
Level 1 Simple, limited communication 1–6 marks	Upper Level 1 4–6 marks	**Content** • Communicates simply • Simple awareness of matching tone, style and register to purpose and audience • Simple vocabulary; simple linguistic devices **Organisation** • Evidence of simple structural features • One or two relevant ideas, simply linked • Random paragraph structure
	Lower Level 1 1–3 marks	**Content** • Limited communication • Occasional sense of matching tone, style and register to purpose and audience • Simple vocabulary **Organisation** • Limited or no evidence of structural features • One or two unlinked ideas • No paragraphs

The mark scheme for Technical Accuracy (AO6) consists of two columns:

- **Level:** There are four levels, with Level 1 at the bottom to Level 4 at the top.

Level	Explanation
Level 4	At this level your writing is extremely accurate. Spelling, punctuation and grammar are almost faultless, and sentences are crafted for impact.
Level 3	At this level your writing is generally accurate. Spelling, punctuation and grammar are mostly secure, and sentences are successfully varied for effect.
Level 2	At this level your writing is sometimes accurate. Spelling, punctuation and grammar contain some errors and sentences are varied for effect but with mixed success.
Level 1	At this level your writing is not very accurate. Spelling, punctuation and grammar contain basic errors and sentences lack variety.

What follows is the Question 5 mark scheme for Technical Accuracy (AO6) for the practice exam paper on pages 6–9.

Level	Skills descriptors
Level 4 13–16 marks	• **Sentence demarcation** is consistently secure and consistently accurate • Wide range of punctuation is used with a high level of accuracy • Uses a full range of appropriate sentence forms for effect • Uses **Standard English** consistently and appropriately with secure control of complex **grammatical structures** • High level of accuracy in spelling, including ambitious vocabulary • Extensive and ambitious use of vocabulary
Level 3 9–12 marks	• Sentence demarcation is mostly secure and mostly accurate • Range of punctuation is used, mostly with success • Uses a variety of sentence forms for effect • Mostly uses Standard English appropriately with mostly controlled grammatical structures • Generally accurate spelling, including complex and **irregular words** • Increasingly sophisticated use of vocabulary
Level 2 5–8 marks	• Sentence demarcation is mostly secure and sometimes accurate • Some control of a range of punctuation • Attempts a variety of sentence forms • Some use of Standard English with some control of agreement • Some accurate spelling of more complex words • Varied use of vocabulary
Level 1 1–4 marks	• Occasional use of sentence demarcation • Some evidence of conscious punctuation • Simple range of sentence forms • Occasional use of Standard English with limited control of agreement • Accurate basic spelling • Simple use of vocabulary

Improving your Question 5 response

Activity 9: Self-assessment

a. Look again at your original response to Question 5. Decide which Content and Organisation (AO5) level your response fits into at the moment based on the overall **quality** of your writing. Use the mark scheme on pages 28–29 to help you make your decision.

b. Think about which parts of your response you could develop in order to improve the Content and Organisation (AO5). Look in particular at how well you have demonstrated your ability to:

- match tone, style and register to purpose and audience
- use effective vocabulary and phrasing
- use effective linguistic devices
- structure your writing effectively
- engage the reader through your choice of subject matter and use of detail
- link and develop your ideas
- use paragraphs and discourse markers effectively.

c. Consider the Upgrade advice in the panel.

d. Now decide which Technical Accuracy (AO6) level your response fits into at the moment based on how accurately it is written. Use the mark scheme on page 30 to help you make your decision.

e. Think about which parts of your response could be improved in terms of Technical Accuracy (AO6). Look in particular at how well you have demonstrated your ability to:

- use accurate spelling
- use accurate punctuation
- use accurate grammar
- vary your sentences effectively.

f. Consider the Upgrade advice in the panel.

g. Rewrite your response with the parts you have developed, corrected and improved, and see if you have now achieved a higher mark.

Key terms

grammatical structure: the arrangement of words, phrases, clauses and sentences to make correct grammatical sense

irregular word: a word that does not follow spelling or phonic 'rules'

sentence demarcation: writing sentences correctly using capital letters and end punctuation, e.g. full stops, question marks and exclamation marks

Standard English: The form of the English language widely accepted as the usual correct form, especially in formal or public situations

Upgrade

AO5

- **Narrate:** When considering how to improve a story, make sure you are clear about the plot (the sequence of events), the setting (where and when the story takes place), the characterisation (who the story is about), the viewpoint (who is narrating the story), the structure (how it begins, what conflict is encountered and how it is resolved) and also the atmosphere (what mood is created).

- **Describe:** When considering how to improve a description, make sure you have included details that appeal to the reader's senses, where appropriate (what they can see, hear, smell and maybe touch and taste in relation to the journey and the discovery), effective vocabulary choices (specific adjectives and adverbs and powerful verbs that bring the description to life) and also imagery such as similes and metaphors.

- **Opening:** Remember to start your story or description in a way that captures your reader's interest immediately.

Upgrade

AO6

Remember, effective communication is the most important skill. If you make too many mistakes in spelling, punctuation and grammar, you will not be able to communicate your ideas effectively.

Progress check

Now you have revisited your original practice exam paper, you are in a position to see which questions you feel confident about and which still need improvement. Look back at the 'What you have to do' sections on pages 10–14 to remind yourself of the skills you need to demonstrate in each question. Then complete the progress check below.

Question 1

	I am confident in this skill.	I have some confidence in this skill.	I need more practice in this skill.
I can find four things in the given lines about the given focus.			

Question 2

	I am confident in this skill.	I have some confidence in this skill.	I need more practice in this skill.
I can choose some examples of language.			
I can write about the effects of my selected examples of language.			
I can use subject terminology to enhance my response.			

Question 3

	I am confident in this skill.	I have some confidence in this skill.	I need more practice in this skill.
I can choose some examples of structural features.			
I can write about the effects of my selected examples of structure.			
I can use subject terminology to enhance my response.			

Question 4

	I am confident in this skill.	I have some confidence in this skill.	I need more practice in this skill.
I can evaluate the ideas in the text.			
I can evaluate the effects of the writer's methods used to convey these ideas.			
I can support my evaluation with textual references.			
I can focus on the given statement.			

Question 5

	I am confident in this skill.	I have some confidence in this skill.	I need more practice in this skill.
I can produce a piece of imaginative writing that communicates to the reader.			
I can match tone, style and register to purpose and audience.			
I can use effective vocabulary and phrasing.			
I can use effective linguistic devices.			
I can structure my writing effectively.			
I can engage the reader through my choice of subject matter and use of detail.			
I can link and develop my ideas.			
I can use paragraphs and discourse markers effectively.			
I can spell accurately.			
I can use punctuation accurately.			
I can use grammar accurately.			
I can vary my sentences effectively.			

Chapter 2: Sample exam paper 1

Source A: 21st-century prose-fiction

This is an extract from the beginning of a novel, Facing the Light *by Adele Geras, published in 2003. Seven-year-old Rilla is visiting Willow Court, a grand old country house belonging to her family. Then one summer evening she makes a discovery that changes everything.*

She is standing at the window. There's not even a breath of wind to move the white curtains   1
and the grass outside lies dry and flat under the last of the sun. Summertime, and early
evening, and she isn't in bed yet. She's nearly eight and it's too soon for sleeping. Everyone
is doing something somewhere else and no one is looking. The shadows of trees are black
on the lawn and the late roses are edged with gold. There's a piece of silvery water glittering   5
through the weeping willow leaves. That's the lake. Swans swim on the lake and she could go
down to the water to see the white birds. No one would know and what you don't know can't
hurt you.   8

She has to go, to flee, across the carpet woven with flowers and twisted trees, and then the   9
door opens and she's in the corridor and it's dark there, always, even when the sun is shining   10
outside, and a thick stillness takes up all the space and spreads down the staircase and she
moves from step to step on tiptoe so as not to disturb it. Paintings on the walls stare at her as
she passes. Still life and landscapes spill strange colours and their own light into the silence
and the portraits scream after her and she can't hear them. The marble floor in the hall is like a
chess board of black and white and she makes sure to jump the black squares because if you   15
don't, something bad is sure to happen, and maybe she just touched one black square on her
way to the garden but that wouldn't count, would it?   17

Then she's on the grass and the air is soft, and she runs as fast as she can down the steps of
the terrace and over the lawn and past all the flowers and between high hedges clipped into
cones and balls and spirals until she reaches the wild garden where the plants brush her skirt,   20
and she's running and running to where the swans always are and they've gone. They have
floated over to the far bank. She can see them. It's not too far away so she starts walking.

Something catches her eye. It's in the reeds and it's like a dark stain in the water and when   23
she gets a little nearer it looks like a sheet or a cloth and there are waterplants and grey-green
willow branches with skinny-finger leaves hiding some of it. If only she can get nearer to where   25
the water meets the bank she can reach in and pull it and see what it is. The water is cool
on her hand and there's something that looks like a foot poking out from under the material.
Could it be someone swimming? No one swims without moving.

Suddenly there's cold all around her and what she doesn't know won't hurt her but she knows
this is wrong. This is bad. She should run and fetch someone but she can't stop her hand from   30
reaching out to the dark cloth that lies on the surface of the lake. She pulls at it and something
heavy comes towards her and the time is stretched so long that the moment goes on for
ever and ever and there's a face with glassy open eyes and pale greenish skin, and she feels
herself starting to scream but no sound comes out and she turns and runs back to the house.
Someone must come. Someone must help, and she runs to call them to bring them and she's   35
screaming and no one can hear her. Wet drowned fingers rise up from the lake and stretch out
over the grass and up into the house to touch her and she will always feel them, even when
she's very old. Now she knows and she can't ever stop knowing.

Section A: Reading

Answer **all** questions in this section.

You are advised to spend about 45 minutes on this section.

0 1 Read again the first part of the source from **lines 1 to 8**.

List **four** things that Rilla can see from the window from this part of the source.

[4 marks]

0 2 Look in detail at this extract from **lines 9 to 17** of the source.

She has to go, to flee, across the carpet woven with flowers and twisted trees, and then the door opens and she's in the corridor and it's dark there, always, even when the sun is shining outside, and a thick stillness takes up all the space and spreads down the staircase and she moves from step to step on tiptoe so as not to disturb it. Paintings on the walls stare at her as she passes. Still life and landscapes spill strange colours and their own light into the silence and the portraits scream after her and she can't hear them. The marble floor in the hall is like a chess board of black and white and she makes sure to jump the black squares because if you don't, something bad is sure to happen, and maybe she just touched one black square on her way to the garden but that wouldn't count, would it?

How does the writer use language here to describe the atmosphere in the house?

You could include the writer's choice of:

- words and phrases
- language features and techniques
- sentence forms.

[8 marks]

0 3 You now need to think about the **whole** of the source.

This text is the opening of a novel.

How has the writer structured the text to interest you as a reader?

You could write about:

- what the writer focuses your attention on at the beginning of the source
- how and why the writer changes this focus as the source develops
- any other structural features that interest you.

[8 marks]

0 4   Focus this part of your answer on the second part of the source from **line 23 to the end**.

A student said, 'This part of the story, where Rilla finds the body in the lake, is really creepy, and I don't think she will ever forget this moment.'

To what extent do you agree?

In your response, you could:

- consider your own impressions of Rilla's reaction to finding the body
- evaluate how the writer creates a creepy atmosphere
- support your response with references to the text.

[20 marks]

Section B: Writing

You are advised to spend about 45 minutes on this section.

Write in full sentences.

You are reminded of the need to plan your answer.

You should leave enough time to check your work at the end.

0 5   An online competition for story writing is being held, and you have decided to enter.

Either

Describe the view from a window as suggested by this picture:

or

Write a story with a twist at the end.

(24 marks for Content and Organisation
16 marks for Technical Accuracy)

[40 marks]

Preparing to practise

Before you attempt this practice exam paper, it is important to remember which skills are being assessed in each question and what you are expected to do to demonstrate those skills. Read through the following and think about the tips for each question.

Question 1

> **Example Exam Question**
>
> **01** Read again the first part of the source from **lines 1 to 8**.
>
> List **four** things that Rilla can see from the window from this part of the source.
>
> **[4 marks]**

You should spend about 3 minutes on this question.

Skills and objectives

- To identify and interpret explicit and implicit information **(AO1)**

What you have to do

- Find four things in the given lines about the given focus. In this practice exam paper you have to find **four** things that **Rilla can see from the window** in **lines 1 to 8**.

> **Tips**
>
> - Make sure you select points from the correct lines.
>
> - Select at least four points.
>
> - Start each point with the focus of the question, e.g. 'Rilla...' or 'She...', so that the points you make are relevant.
>
> - Retrieve points rather than trying to interpret the source – in case you actually misinterpret the text!

Question 2

Example Exam Question

02 Look in detail at **lines 9 to 17** of the source.

How does the writer use language here to describe the atmosphere in the house?

You could include the writer's choice of:

- words and phrases
- language features and techniques
- sentence forms.

[8 marks]

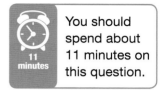

You should spend about 11 minutes on this question.

Skills and objectives

- To analyse how the writer's use of language achieves effects **(AO2)**

What you have to do

- Choose some examples of language. In this practice exam paper you have to focus on language **in lines 9 to 17** used **to describe the atmosphere in the house**.

- Write about the effects of your selected examples of language.

- Use subject terminology to enhance your response.

Tips

- Make sure you select examples of language from the correct lines.

- Remember that the most important part of this question is the **quality** of what you write about the **effects of language**. Your comments have to be **precise** and **contextualised** in order to achieve Level 3 and above.

- Notice the word 'could' in the question. You 'could' write about words and phrases, language features and techniques, or sentence forms, but you don't have to write about all of them.

- Zoom in on individual words and phrases to analyse their effects.

Question 3

Example Exam Question

03 You now need to think about the **whole** of the source.

This text is the opening of a novel.

How has the writer structured the text to interest you as a reader?

You could write about:

• what the writer focuses your attention on at the beginning of the source

• how and why the writer changes this focus as the source develops

• any other structural features that interest you.

[8 marks]

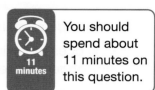

You should spend about 11 minutes on this question.

Skills and objectives

• To analyse how the writer's use of structure achieves effects **(AO2)**

What you have to do

• Choose some examples of structural features from the **whole** source.

• Write about the effects of your selected examples of structure.

• Use subject terminology to enhance your response.

Tips

• Make sure you select examples of structure from the **whole** source.

• Remember that the most important part of this question is the **quality** of what you write about the **effects of structural features**. Your comments have to be **precise** and **contextualised** in order to achieve Level 3 and above.

• Consider 'Where? What? Why?' and ask yourself the question: 'How does reading about this **at this point** add to my understanding of the whole source?'

• Look at the sequencing, structural shifts and movement through the text, and write about the possible reasons behind these structural choices. Try to make links and connections between different parts of the text.

Question 4

Example Exam Question

04 Focus this part of your answer on the second part of the source from **line 23 to the end**.

A student said, 'This part of the story, where Rilla finds the body in the lake, is really creepy, and I don't think she will ever forget this moment.'

To what extent do you agree?

In your response, you could:

- consider your own impressions of Rilla's reaction to finding the body
- evaluate how the writer creates a creepy atmosphere
- support your response with references to the text.

[20 marks]

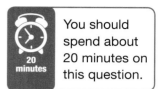 You should spend about 20 minutes on this question.

Skills and objectives

- To evaluate the text critically and support this with appropriate textual references **(AO4)**

What you have to do

- Evaluate the ideas in the text. In this practice exam paper you are directed to the second part of the source **from line 23**. You have to consider **your own impressions of Rilla's reaction to finding the body** and also **how the writer creates a creepy atmosphere**.

- Evaluate the effects of the writer's methods used to convey these ideas.

- Support your evaluation with textual references.

- Focus on the given statement. In this practice exam paper the focus is **the creepy atmosphere** and **whether or not Rilla will ever forget the moment she finds the body**.

Tips

- Make sure you focus your evaluation on the correct lines.

- Think of evaluation as the **interpretation** of content (the 'what') and **analysis** of method ('the how') in relation to a given statement.

- Make sure you evaluate the 'how' as well as the 'what'.

- Remember that the most important part of this question is the **quality** of what you write about **both the ideas and the writer's methods** used to convey these ideas. Your comments have to be **precise** and **contextualised** in order to achieve Level 3 and above.

- There are no right or wrong answers – before you start to write, separate the different elements of the question, decide if you agree, partially agree or disagree, and then select relevant evidence from the text to support your opinions.

Question 5

Example Exam Question

05 An online competition for story writing is being held, and you have decided to enter.

Either

Describe the view from a window as suggested by the picture.

or

Write a story with a twist at the end.

[40 marks]

You should spend about 35 minutes on this question: 5 minutes to plan, 25 minutes to write and 5 minutes to check at the end.

Skills and objectives

* To communicate effectively and imaginatively in an appropriate style according to purpose and audience **(AO5)**
* To organise information and ideas, using structural and grammatical features **(AO5)**
* To write clearly and accurately **(AO6)**

What you have to do

* Produce a piece of imaginative writing that communicates to the reader.
* Demonstrate the ability to match tone, style and register to purpose and audience.
* Use effective vocabulary and phrasing.
* Use effective linguistic devices.
* Structure your writing effectively.
* Engage the reader through your choice of subject matter and use of detail.
* Link and develop your ideas.
* Use paragraphs and discourse markers effectively.
* Write accurately.

Tips

* Remember that what is being assessed is the **quality** of your writing. You have to communicate **clearly** in order to reach Level 3 or above.
* Take time to plan your response before you start writing, e.g. if you chose the narrative option, think about plot, setting, characterisation, viewpoint, structure and atmosphere.
* Adopt a quality rather than quantity approach – a shorter, crafted response is better than a longer, rambling one.
* Leave time at the end to proofread your response, and correct and improve where possible.

Activity 1: Answering the practice exam paper

Using all the tips you have read above, complete the practice exam paper on pages 34–37.

Unpicking the mark scheme

A mark scheme is used to assess the quality of your response for each question. Unpicking the mark scheme can show you how the levels and marks are awarded. This can help you to improve the quality of your work because you will understand exactly what is expected of you in each question.

Question 1 mark scheme

Example Exam Question

01 List **four** things that Rilla can see from the window from **lines 1 to 8** of the source.

[4 marks]

Question 1 is different from all the other Reading questions because it is the only question where the answers are either right or wrong. You are awarded 1 mark for each correct point, up to a total of 4 marks.

What follows is the Question 1 mark scheme for the practice exam paper on pages 34–37.

> Indicative content; students may include:
> - Rilla can see dry grass.
> - She can see trees.
> - She can see that the sun is going down.
> - She can see there are black shadows on the lawn.
> - She can see roses that have gold edges.
> - She can see a lake.
> - She can see that the water in the lake is silvery.
> - She can see a weeping willow tree.
>
> Or any other valid responses that you are able to verify by checking the source.

These are not the only correct answers. The mark scheme includes the instruction 'Or any other valid responses that you are able to verify by checking the source' because there may be other correct points that are not listed, e.g. 'She can see that the water is glittering' would also be awarded 1 mark.

Other mark scheme instructions for Question 1 can also help you to be clear about how to answer this question:

- You can only be awarded a mark if you select from the correct lines and what you select is correct.

- You can only be awarded a mark if what you select is relevant, i.e. something Rilla can see.

- You can use the exact words from the text or you can use your own words.
- If you include more than one point in a line, you will be awarded a mark for each point, as long as the point is relevant.
- If you copy out the whole section word for word, you will not be awarded any marks because you have not demonstrated the ability to select relevant points.

Improving your Question 1 response

Activity 2: Self-assessment

a. Look again at your original response to Question 1. Decide how many marks you would be awarded at the moment. Use the mark scheme on page 43 to help you make your decision.

b. Reread lines 1 to 8 of the source. Using the mark scheme as a guide, circle each individual point about what Rilla can see as you read.

c. Choose which additional points you will add to your response and write them out.

d. Look at your whole response and see if you have now achieved a higher mark.

Tip

In a question where you need to find particular details, circling points as you read can be helpful when you then come to write your answer out.

Question 2 mark scheme

Example Exam Question

02 How does the writer use language in **lines 9 to 17** to describe the atmosphere in the house?

You could include the writer's choice of:

- words and phrases
- language features and techniques
- sentence forms.

[8 marks]

The mark scheme for Question 2 consists of three columns:

- **Level:** There are four levels, from Level 1 at the bottom to Level 4 at the top. Each level has key words that sum up the quality of responses in that level.

Level	Key words	Explanation
Level 4	'Detailed' and 'perceptive'	This means you are seeing meaning deep below the surface and your analysis of the writer's use of language is insightful and astute.
Level 3	'Clear' and 'relevant'	This means your explanation of the writer's use of language is developed, precise and contextualised.
Level 2	'Some understanding and comment'	This means you are trying to comment on the writer's use of language and you are having some success, but what you are saying is undeveloped and not yet clear.
Level 1	'Simple' and 'limited'	This means what you are saying about the writer's use of language is basic and obvious.

- **Skills descriptors:** This column shows the skills being assessed in Question 2. Your response is placed in a level according to how well you have demonstrated the key skill – writing about the effects of the writer's choice of language. How well you demonstrate the other skills determines your mark within that level.

- **Indicative standard:** This column shows the **quality** of response that is expected at each level. It does not show the correct answer in terms of content because you may not select the same examples of language, but the quality of your analysis of language will be matched against the quality of these indicative standard responses.

What follows is the Question 2 mark scheme for the practice exam paper on pages 34–37. Because the most important part of this question is the **quality** of what you write about the effects of language, this key skill has been highlighted so that you can trace the thread through the mark scheme levels to see the progression from Level 1 to Level 4.

Level	Skills descriptors	Indicative standard
Level 4 Detailed, perceptive analysis 7–8 marks	Shows detailed and perceptive understanding of language: • Analyses the effects of the writer's choices of language • Selects a range of judicious textual detail • Makes sophisticated and accurate use of subject terminology	The writer uses rather unsettling language to describe the atmosphere in the house. The corridor is 'dark' and a 'thick stillness takes up all the space and spreads down the staircase'. This image suggests that the air, something that should be intangible, has become almost a solid being in its own right: it is a heavy, overbearing and impenetrable force. The lengthy sentences with multiple clauses reflect the ever-growing nature of this entity as it advances, and the use of sibilance helps to magnify the insidious atmosphere that is created and also Rilla's fear. Furthermore, the writer personifies the paintings on the wall. They 'stare at her as she passes' as if they are studying her, deliberately fixing their gaze on her and her alone in an intimidating and menacing way.
Level 3 Clear, relevant explanation 5–6 marks	Shows clear understanding of language: • Explains clearly the effects of the writer's choices of language • Selects a range of relevant textual detail • Makes clear and accurate use of subject terminology	The writer uses quite disturbing language to describe the atmosphere in the house, e.g. the corridor is 'dark' and a 'thick stillness takes up all the space and spreads down the staircase'. This metaphor suggests that the air is dense and absolutely silent, almost reaching out for Rilla as it expands. When she runs down the staircase, the paintings 'stare at her as she passes'. The use of personification here suggests the pictures have a life of their own – they seem to be watching Rilla and gazing intensely at her in a threatening way as she passes by.

Level	Skills descriptors	Indicative standard
Level 2 Some understanding and comment 3–4 marks	Shows some understanding of language: • Attempts to comment on the effect of language • Selects some appropriate textual detail • Makes some use of subject terminology, mainly appropriately	The writer uses words like 'dark' and also the language technique of personification to describe the atmosphere in the house as scary. It says a 'thick stillness takes up all the space', which shows us that everything is quiet and you could cut the air with a knife. Then the paintings 'stare at her as she passes', so it's like they are alive, which is creepy and Rilla must be scared.
Level 1 Simple, limited comment 1–2 marks	Shows simple awareness of language: • Offers simple comment on the effect of language • Selects simple reference(s) or textual detail(s) • Makes simple use of subject terminology, not always appropriately	The house is 'dark' and there is a 'thick stillness'. These words mean it's really bad in the house. The writer says the paintings 'stare at her as she passes', so when Rilla goes down the stairs the pictures look at her. This makes the atmosphere sound horrible.

Activity 3: Tracking levels of response

a. To help you see the progression more clearly, choose one comment in the highlighted Level 1 indicative standard response, e.g. 'so when Rilla goes down the stairs the pictures look at her'. Copy it out, and then write down the improved version of this comment shown at Level 2, Level 3, and Level 4. Look at the quality of comment demonstrated in each level.

b. Think about how you could improve your own response.

Improving your Question 2 response

Activity 4: Self-assessment

a. Look again at your original response to Question 2. Decide which level your response fits into at the moment. Use the mark scheme on pages 45–46 to help you make your decision.

b. Think about which parts of your response you could develop in order to improve it. Look in particular at the **quality** of what you have written about the effects of language.

- Look at the difference in the skills descriptor bullets at different levels. For example, a response needs to develop from 'attempts to comment' to 'explains clearly' in order to move from Level 2 to Level 3.

- Work in steps: What word/phrase/language feature have you selected? How has the writer used it to create an effect? Why might the writer have intended this effect?

- The better you link these elements together, the more successful your response should be.

c. Consider the Upgrade advice in the panel.

d. Rewrite your response with the parts you have developed, and see if you have now achieved a higher mark.

Upgrade

- Think about the effect of the writer's choice of individual words, e.g. the carpet is 'woven with flowers and twisted trees'. Why is the word 'twisted' particularly successful?

- When discussing the effects of language, remember it is important to consider the context in which the words and phrases are used, and to be precise when commenting on effect.

- Using a phrase such as 'This suggests...' shows that you are beginning to interpret the effect of the writer's language used to convey the atmosphere in the house. Other useful phrases include: 'This means...', 'This lets us know...', 'This indicates...', 'This implies...' and 'This makes me think...'.

Question 3 mark scheme

03 This text is the opening of a novel.

How has the writer structured the text to interest you as a reader?

You could write about:

- what the writer focuses your attention on at the beginning of the source
- how and why the writer changes this focus as the source develops
- any other structural features that interest you.

[8 marks]

The mark scheme for Question 3 consists of three columns:

- **Level:** There are four levels, from Level 1 at the bottom to Level 4 at the top. Each level has key words that sum up the quality of responses in that level.

Level	Key words	Explanation
Level 4	'Detailed' and 'perceptive'	This means you are seeing meaning deep below the surface and your analysis of the writer's use of structure is insightful and astute.
Level 3	'Clear' and 'relevant'	This means your explanation of the writer's use of structure is developed, precise and contextualised.
Level 2	'Some understanding and comment'	This means you are trying to comment on the writer's use of structure and you are having some success, but what you are saying is undeveloped and not yet clear.
Level 1	'Simple' and 'limited'	This means what you are saying about the writer's use of structure is basic and obvious.

- **Skills descriptors:** This column shows the skills being assessed in Question 3. Your response is placed in a level according to how well you have demonstrated the key skill – writing about the effects of the writer's choice of structural features. How well you demonstrate the other skills determines your mark within that level.

- **Indicative standard:** This column shows the **quality** of response that is expected at each level. It does not show the correct answer in terms of content because you may not select the same examples of structure, but the quality of your analysis of structure will be matched against the quality of these indicative standard responses.

What follows is the Question 3 mark scheme for the practice exam paper on pages 34–37. Because the most important part of this question is the **quality** of what you write about the effects of structural features, this key skill has been highlighted so that you can trace the thread through the mark scheme levels to see the progression from Level 1 to Level 4.

Level	Skills descriptors	Indicative standard
Level 4 Detailed, perceptive analysis 7–8 marks	Shows detailed and perceptive understanding of structural features: • Analyses the effects of the writer's choices of structural features • Selects a range of judicious examples • Makes sophisticated and accurate use of subject terminology	The atmosphere of the text changes from the idyllic calm stillness of a summer evening at the beginning of the source, when Rilla is in her bedroom and there is 'not even a breath of wind to move the white curtains', to the horror at the end when she discovers a body with 'glassy open eyes' in the lake. The reader observes the contrast between the inside, where a seven-year-old girl can be safe and protected, and what happens when she ventures outside, where the evil of the real, grown-up world lurks. The writer foreshadows the shock ending in the transitional paragraph that links the inside/outside locations when Rilla is running through the corridors and staircase of the house. She crosses the hall, with its floor 'like a chess board', and tries to avoid the black squares as she considers them unlucky. It says 'maybe she just touched one black square on her way to the garden but that wouldn't count, would it?' At this point, her doubt becomes the reader's certainty: this is more than just a superstitious game and something dreadful is about to happen to her.
Level 3 Clear, relevant explanation 5–6 marks	Shows clear understanding of structural features: • Explains clearly the effects of the writer's choices of structural features • Selects a range of relevant examples • Makes clear and accurate use of subject terminology	At the beginning Rilla is in her bedroom, looking out of the window at the 'silvery water' of the lake, and at the end she is outside and finds a body in the water. The atmosphere at the start is the peacefulness of a 'summertime' evening, but later there is horror. This change in mood is foreshadowed by the writer when Rilla tries to jump over the black squares of the 'chess board' hall floor because she thinks they're unlucky. It says 'maybe she just touched one black square on her way to the garden but that wouldn't count, would it?', which is important because it suggests to the reader that her superstitious belief of something bad happening is about to come true.
Level 2 Some understanding and comment 3–4 marks	Shows some understanding of structural features: • Attempts to comment on the effect of structural features • Selects some appropriate examples • Makes some use of subject terminology, mainly appropriately	The writer focuses on Rilla inside her bedroom at the start, and we learn that she wants to go to see the swans. Then our focus switches to the corridors and staircase and then Rilla goes outside. It sounds lovely at the start but at the end it's horrible. We know something bad is going to happen because she thinks standing on the black squares on the hall floor is unlucky, and says 'maybe she just touched one black square on her way to the garden but that wouldn't count, would it?', but it obviously does.
Level 1 Simple, limited comment 1–2 marks	Shows simple awareness of structural features: • Offers simple comment on the effect of structure • Selects simple reference(s) or example(s) • Makes simple use of subject terminology, not always appropriately	At the beginning we see Rilla in her bedroom and then she goes to see the swans. It's all nice at the start but at the end it's bad, so it goes from inside and nice to outside and bad.

Activity 5: Tracking levels of response

a. To help you see the progression more clearly, choose one comment in the highlighted Level 1 indicative standard response, e.g. 'it's all nice at the start but at the end it's bad'. Copy it out, and then write down the improved version of this comment shown at Level 2, Level 3, and Level 4. Look at the quality of comment demonstrated in each level.

b. Think about how you could improve your own response.

Improving your Question 3 response

Activity 6: Self-assessment

a. Look again at your original response to Question 3. Decide which level your response fits into at the moment. Use the mark scheme on page 49 to help you make your decision.

b. Think about which parts of your response you could develop in order to improve it. Look in particular at the **quality** of what you have written about the effects of structural features.

- Look at the difference in the skills descriptor bullets at different levels. For example, a response needs to develop from 'attempts to comment' to 'explains clearly' in order to move from Level 2 to Level 3.

- Work in steps. Consider 'Where? What? Why?' and ask yourself the question 'How does reading about this **at this point** add to my understanding of the whole source?'

- The better you link these elements together, the more successful your answer should be.

c. Consider the Upgrade advice in the panel.

d. Rewrite your response with the parts you have developed, and see if you have now achieved a higher mark.

Upgrade

- Remember to look at the sequencing, structural shifts and movement through the text, and write about the possible reasons behind these structural choices.
- Structural shifts that are relevant to this text include:
  - zooming in from something big to something much smaller
  - shifting between different times and places
  - the introduction of a new character at a significant point
  - combining external actions with internal thoughts
  - developing and reiterating, i.e. focusing on an important idea and repeating it
- Remember to make links and connections between these different parts of the text.

Question 4 mark scheme

Example Exam Question

04 A student said, 'This part of the story (line 23 to the end), where Rilla finds the body in the lake, is really creepy, and I don't think she will ever forget this moment.'

To what extent do you agree?

In your response, you could:

- consider your own impressions of Rilla's reaction to finding the body
- evaluate how the writer creates a creepy atmosphere
- support your response with references to the text.

[20 marks]

The mark scheme for Question 4 consists of three columns:

- **Level:** There are four levels, from Level 1 at the bottom to Level 4 at the top. Each level has key words that sum up the quality of responses in that level.

Level	Key words	Explanation
Level 4	'Detailed' and 'perceptive'	This means you are seeing meaning deep below the surface and your evaluation of ideas and/or the writer's methods is insightful and astute.
Level 3	'Clear' and 'relevant'	This means your evaluation of ideas and/or the writer's methods is developed, precise and contextualised.
Level 2	'Some evaluation'	This means you are trying to evaluate ideas and/or the writer's methods and that you are having some success, but what you are saying is undeveloped and not yet clear.
Level 1	'Simple' and 'limited'	This means your evaluation of ideas and/or the writer's methods is basic and obvious.

- **Skills descriptors:** This column shows the skills being assessed in Question 4. Your response is placed in a level according to how well you have demonstrated the key skills – writing about the ideas and the writer's methods used to convey these ideas. How well you demonstrate the other skills determines your mark within that level.

- **Indicative standard:** This column shows the **quality** of response that is expected at each level. It does not show the correct answer in terms of content because you may not evaluate the same ideas or the same writer's methods, but the quality of your evaluation will be matched against the quality of these indicative standard responses.

What follows is the Question 4 mark scheme for the practice exam paper on pages 34–37. Because the most important part of this question is the **quality** of your evaluation of ideas and the writer's methods used to convey these ideas, these key skills have been highlighted so that you can trace the threads through the mark scheme levels to see the progression from Level 1 to Level 4. Green highlighting shows comments evaluating the relevant ideas; yellow highlighting shows comments on the writer's methods.

Level	Skills descriptors	Indicative standard
Level 4 Detailed, perceptive evaluation 16–20 marks	Shows detailed and perceptive evaluation: • Evaluates critically and in detail the effect(s) on the reader • Shows perceptive understanding of writer's methods • Selects a range of judicious textual detail • Develops a convincing and critical response to the focus of the statement	Rilla tries to rationalise the unusual things she sees and impose a logical explanation from within her limited experience of life – the 'dark stain' resembles 'a sheet or a cloth' and as she moves nearer, 'something that looks like a foot' is probably 'someone swimming'. However, the fact that Rilla questions herself ('Could it be...?') creates an element of uncertainty and suggests to the reader that deep down, she is aware of her own naivety – this is far worse than anything she has ever encountered. The writer creates a creepy atmosphere by describing not only the physicality of the body using gruesome language – 'glassy open eyes and pale greenish skin'– but also what Rilla sees in her imagination as she is running away, which is worse. The 'wet drowned fingers', with their ability to 'rise up', 'stretch' and 'touch' personify all that is evil into the one body part capable of touching and destroying a little girl. The recurring motif of 'what you don't know can't hurt you' from earlier in the text is echoed here with the finality of 'Now she knows and she can't ever stop knowing.' The innocence of youth has vanished and Rilla's life will forever be tainted by this devastating discovery.

Level	Skills descriptors	Indicative standard
Level 3 Clear, relevant evaluation 11–15 marks	Shows clear and relevant evaluation: • Evaluates clearly the effect(s) on the reader • Shows clear understanding of writer's methods • Selects a range of relevant textual references • Makes a clear and relevant response to the focus of the statement	Rilla tries to suggest reasonable explanations for everything she sees. She says the 'dark stain' looks like 'a sheet or a cloth' and then, as she moves nearer, 'something that looks like a foot' could be 'someone swimming'. These are the innocent interpretations of a seven-year-old child. She knows she should fetch help, but she's not supposed to be out at the lake and the lure of the object right in front of her is too strong to resist. The writer creates a creepy atmosphere as Rilla runs away by saying 'wet drowned fingers rise up from the lake'. Personifying the body shows the depth of Rilla's fear because she thinks it is alive and has the power to get her. She thinks she will forever be haunted by these fingers, 'even when she's very old', so I agree she will never forget this moment because it has changed her life.
Level 2 Some evaluation 6–10 marks	Shows some attempts at evaluation: • Makes some evaluative comment(s) on effect(s) on the reader • Shows some understanding of writer's methods • Selects some appropriate textual reference(s) • Makes some response to the focus of the statement	At first Rilla sees a 'dark stain' and says it looks like 'a sheet or a cloth'. She is trying to think of things she knows as she wouldn't be expecting a body. Then she goes nearer and sees 'something that looks like a foot'. The writer makes it sound creepy here because a foot is worse than a sheet or a cloth. Rilla tells herself it's 'someone swimming' because that makes sense to her, but I think deep down she knows it's not. She should get help but she might get told off for being there. I agree she will never forget this moment because she says she will always feel the 'wet drowned fingers'.
Level 1 Simple, limited comment 1–5 marks	Shows simple, limited evaluation: • Makes simple, limited evaluative comment(s) on effect(s) on the reader • Shows limited understanding of writer's methods • Selects simple, limited textual reference(s) • Makes a simple, limited response to the focus of the statement	Rilla sees 'something that looks like a foot' and says it's 'someone swimming', but obviously that's not true. Then she runs away so I think she is scared. The writer makes it sound creepy by saying there are 'wet drowned fingers' and this is horrible. I agree she will never forget this moment because no one would forget finding a body.

Activity 7: Tracking levels of response

a. To help you see the progression more clearly, choose one comment in the highlighted Level 1 indicative standard response, e.g. 'The writer makes it sound creepy...'. Copy it out, and then write down the improved version of this comment shown at Level 2, Level 3, and Level 4. Look at the quality of comment demonstrated in each level.

b. Think about how you could improve your own response.

Improving your Question 4 response

Activity 8: Self-assessment

a. Look again at your original response to Question 4. Decide which level your response fits into at the moment. Use the mark scheme on pages 52–53 to help you make your decision.

b. Think about which parts of your response you could develop in order to improve it. Look in particular at the **quality** of your evaluation of ideas and the writer's methods used to convey these ideas.

- Look at the difference in the skills descriptor bullets at different levels. For example, a response needs to develop from 'shows some understanding' to 'shows clear understanding' in order to move from Level 2 to Level 3.

- Work in steps: What relevant ideas have you identified to evaluate? What methods has the writer used to convey those ideas?

- The better you link these elements together, the more successful your answer should be.

c. Consider the Upgrade advice in the panel.

d. Rewrite your response with the parts you have developed, and see if you have now achieved a higher mark.

Upgrade

- Look for evidence that the atmosphere is creepy, plus evidence that Rilla will never forget this moment and also evidence that she might forget this moment. Then decide whether or not you agree, partially agree or disagree, with the given statement.

- As part of your evaluation, remember you are expected to interpret, as well as identify, the relevant ideas.

- Make sure you also evaluate the effects of the writer's methods used to convey these ideas. In this text you could consider not only language and structure but also narrative voice.

Question 5 mark scheme

Example Exam Question

05 Either	Describe the view from a window as suggested by the picture.
or	Write a story with a twist at the end.

[40 marks]

In Question 5 you will be assessed on:

• Content and Organisation **(AO5)**

• Technical Accuracy **(AO6)**.

So the mark scheme for Question 5 is divided into two parts.

The mark scheme for Content and Organisation (AO5) consists of three columns:

• **Level:** There are four levels, from Level 1 at the bottom to Level 4 at the top. Each level has key words that sum up the quality of responses in that level.

Level	Key words	Explanation
Level 4	'Compelling, convincing communication'	This means that your writing is crafted for impact. Ideas are linked in a confident, seamless manner and form a unified whole. Your reader is gripped and emotionally involved in the outcome.
Level 3	'Consistent, clear communication'	This means that your writing is shaped, fluent and makes sense as a whole. Ideas are effectively linked, developed and relevant to purpose. Your reader is interested in finding out what happens.
Level 2	'Some successful communication'	This means that your writing makes sense at times. Some ideas are linked but others may be illogical or undeveloped. Your reader is interested in parts but loses the thread of what you are saying.
Level 1	'Simple, limited communication'	This means that your writing doesn't always make sense. Ideas are basic and may be rambling and not well organised. Your reader struggles to follow what you are saying.

• **Sub-level:** Each of the four levels is broken down into an upper level and a lower level. To move into an upper level you have to demonstrate a higher level of skill or sustain the skills in the lower half of the level.

• **Skills descriptors:** This column shows the skills being assessed in Question 5. Your response is placed in a level according to how well you have demonstrated the key skill – overall communication. How well you demonstrate the other skills determines your mark within that level.

What follows is the Question 5 mark scheme for Content and Organisation (AO5) for the practice exam paper on pages 34–37. Because the most important part of this question is the **quality** of your overall communication, this key skill has been highlighted so that you can trace the thread through the mark scheme levels to see the progression from Level 1 to Level 4.

Level	Sub-level	Skills descriptors
Level 4 Compelling, convincing communication 19–24 marks	Upper Level 4 22–24 marks	**Content** • Communication is convincing and compelling • Tone, style and register are assuredly matched to purpose and audience • Extensive and ambitious vocabulary with sustained crafting of linguistic devices **Organisation** • Varied and inventive use of structural features • Writing is compelling, incorporating a range of convincing and complex ideas • Fluently linked paragraphs with seamlessly integrated discourse markers
	Lower Level 4 19–21 marks	**Content** • Communication is convincing • Tone, style and register are convincingly matched to purpose and audience • Extensive vocabulary with conscious crafting of linguistic devices **Organisation** • Varied and effective structural features • Writing is highly engaging with a range of developed complex ideas • Consistently coherent use of paragraphs with integrated discourse markers
Level 3 Consistent, clear communication 13–18 marks	Upper Level 3 16–18 marks	**Content** • Communication is consistently clear • Tone, style and register are clearly and consistently matched to purpose and audience • Increasingly sophisticated vocabulary and phrasing, chosen for effect with a range of successful linguistic devices **Organisation** • Effective use of structural features • Writing is engaging, using a range of clear connected ideas • Coherent paragraphs with integrated discourse markers

Level	Sub-level	Skills descriptors
	Lower Level 3 13–15 marks	**Content** • Communication is generally clear • Tone, style and register are generally matched to purpose and audience • Vocabulary clearly chosen for effect and appropriate use of linguistic devices **Organisation** • Usually effective use of structural features • Writing is engaging, with a range of connected ideas • Usually coherent paragraphs with range of discourse markers
Level 2 Some successful communication 7–12 marks	Upper Level 2 10–12 marks	**Content** • Communicates with some sustained success • Some sustained attempt to match tone, style and register to purpose and audience • Conscious use of vocabulary with some use of linguistic devices **Organisation** • Some use of structural features • Increasing variety of linked and relevant ideas • Some use of paragraphs and some use of discourse markers
	Lower Level 2 7–9 marks	**Content** • Communicates with some success • Attempts to match tone, style and register to purpose and audience • Begins to vary vocabulary with some use of linguistic devices **Organisation** • Attempts to use structural features • Some linked and relevant ideas • Attempts to write in paragraphs with some discourse markers, not always appropriate
Level 1 Simple, limited communication 1–6 marks	Upper Level 1 4–6 marks	**Content** • Communicates simply • Simple awareness of matching tone, style and register to purpose and audience • Simple vocabulary; simple linguistic devices **Organisation** • Evidence of simple structural features • One or two relevant ideas, simply linked • Random paragraph structure
	Lower Level 1 1–3 marks	**Content** • Limited communication • Occasional sense of matching tone, style and register to purpose and audience • Simple vocabulary **Organisation** • Limited or no evidence of structural features • One or two unlinked ideas • No paragraphs

The mark scheme for Technical Accuracy (AO6) consists of two columns:

- **Level:** There are four levels, from Level 1 at the bottom to Level 4 at the top.

Level	Explanation
Level 4	At this level your writing is extremely accurate. Spelling, punctuation and grammar are almost faultless, and sentences are crafted for impact.
Level 3	At this level your writing is generally accurate. Spelling, punctuation and grammar are mostly secure, and sentences are successfully varied for effect.
Level 2	At this level your writing is sometimes accurate. Spelling, punctuation and grammar contain some errors and sentences are varied for effect but with mixed success.
Level 1	At this level your writing is not very accurate. Spelling, punctuation and grammar contain basic errors and sentences lack variety.

What follows is the Question 5 mark scheme for Technical Accuracy (AO6) for the practice exam paper on pages 34–37.

Level	Skills descriptors
Level 4 13–16 marks	- Sentence demarcation is consistently secure and consistently accurate - Wide range of punctuation is used with a high level of accuracy - Uses a full range of appropriate sentence forms for effect - Uses Standard English consistently and appropriately with secure control of complex grammatical structures - High level of accuracy in spelling, including ambitious vocabulary - Extensive and ambitious use of vocabulary
Level 3 9–12 marks	- Sentence demarcation is mostly secure and mostly accurate - Range of punctuation is used, mostly with success - Uses a variety of sentence forms for effect - Mostly uses Standard English appropriately with mostly controlled grammatical structures - Generally accurate spelling, including complex and irregular words - Increasingly sophisticated use of vocabulary
Level 2 5–8 marks	- Sentence demarcation is mostly secure and sometimes accurate - Some control of a range of punctuation - Attempts a variety of sentence forms - Some use of Standard English with some control of agreement - Some accurate spelling of more complex words - Varied use of vocabulary

Level	Skills descriptors
Level 1 1–4 marks	• Occasional use of sentence demarcation • Some evidence of conscious punctuation • Simple range of sentence forms • Occasional use of Standard English with limited control of agreement • Accurate basic spelling • Simple use of vocabulary

Improving your Question 5 response

Activity 9: Self-assessment

a. Look again at your original response to Question 5. Decide which Content and Organisation (AO5) level your response fits into at the moment based on the overall **quality** of your writing. Use the mark scheme on pages 56–57 to help you make your decision.

b. Think about which parts of your response you could develop in order to improve the Content and Organisation (AO5). Look in particular at how well you have demonstrated your ability to:

- match tone, style and register to purpose and audience
- use effective vocabulary and phrasing
- use effective linguistic devices
- structure your writing effectively
- engage the reader through your choice of subject matter and use of detail
- link and develop your ideas
- use paragraphs and discourse markers effectively.

c. Consider the Upgrade advice in the panel.

d. Now decide which Technical Accuracy (AO6) level your response fits into at the moment based on how accurately it is written. Use the mark scheme on pages 58–59 to help you make your decision.

e. Think about which parts of your response could be improved in terms of Technical Accuracy (AO6). Look in particular at how well you have demonstrated your ability to:

- use accurate spelling
- use accurate punctuation
- use accurate grammar
- vary your sentences effectively.

f. Consider the Upgrade advice in the panel on the following page.

g. Rewrite your response with the parts you have developed, corrected and improved, and see if you have now achieved a higher mark.

Upgrade

AO6
Remember, effective communication is the most important skill. If you make too many mistakes in spelling, punctuation and grammar, you will not be able to communicate your ideas effectively.

Upgrade

AO5

- **Describe:** When considering how to improve a description, make sure you have included details that appeal to the reader's senses, where appropriate, effective vocabulary choices and also imagery such as similes and metaphors.
- **Narrate:** When considering how to improve a story, make sure you are clear about the plot (the sequence of events), the setting, the characterisation (who the story is about), the viewpoint (who is narrating the story), the structure (how it begins, what conflict is encountered and how it is resolved) and also the atmosphere (what mood is created).
- **Opening:** Remember to start a story or description in a way that captures your reader's interest immediately.

Progress check

Now you have revisited your original practice exam paper, you are in a position to see which questions you feel confident about and which still need improvement. Look back at the 'What you have to do' sections on pages 38–42 to remind yourself of the skills you need to demonstrate in each question. Then complete the progress check below.

Question 1

	I am confident in this skill.	I have some confidence in this skill.	I need more practice in this skill.
I can find four things in the given lines about the given focus.			

Question 2

	I am confident in this skill.	I have some confidence in this skill.	I need more practice in this skill.
I can choose some examples of language.			
I can write about the effects of my selected examples of language.			
I can use subject terminology to enhance my response.			

Question 3

	I am confident in this skill.	I have some confidence in this skill.	I need more practice in this skill.
I can choose some examples of structural features.			
I can write about the effects of my selected examples of structure.			
I can use subject terminology to enhance my response.			

Question 4

	I am confident in this skill.	I have some confidence in this skill.	I need more practice in this skill.
I can evaluate the ideas in the text.			
I can evaluate the effects of the writer's methods used to convey these ideas.			
I can support my evaluation with textual references.			
I can focus on the given statement.			

Question 5

	I am confident in this skill.	I have some confidence in this skill.	I need more practice in this skill.
I can produce a piece of imaginative writing that communicates to the reader.			
I can match tone, style and register to purpose and audience.			
I can use effective vocabulary and phrasing.			
I can use effective linguistic devices.			
I can structure my writing effectively.			
I can engage the reader through my choice of subject matter and use of detail.			
I can link and develop my ideas.			
I can use paragraphs and discourse markers effectively.			
I can spell accurately.			
I can use punctuation accurately.			
I can use grammar accurately.			
I can vary my sentences effectively.			

Chapter 3: Sample exam paper 2

Source A: 21st-century literary non-fiction

This is an extract from a newspaper article, 'Through the Pyrenees on the Little Yellow Train' by Gavin Bell, published in 2016. It is one of a series of newspaper articles published in The Telegraph *on the subject of rail journeys. The writer describes travelling through the mountains of France.*

The road to fairyland is quicker, but the railway is more fun. It begins at a medieval fortified town deep in a French mountain valley, and climbs to a plateau in the sky where wildflowers bloom and eagles fly.   1

The Little Yellow Train of the eastern Pyrenees is a magical trip through time and space that has been defying both with daring engineering and merry toot-toots of its whistle for more than a   5
century.   6

In 1925 the Scottish artist Charles Rennie Mackintosh and his wife travelled on the train to a 17th-century castle among the high peaks, and were enchanted by spring meadows ablaze with mountain flowers. He called it fairyland, and it became their favourite summer haunt, where they gathered bouquets of flowers for him to paint in watercolours.   10

Most of the original carriages that entered service in 1909 are still trundling along the narrow-gauge electric line that runs for almost 40 miles from Villefranche to the Spanish border, via the highest railway station in France at above 5,000 feet.

The engineers who designed it clearly had an adventurous spirit. The line snakes improbably through chasms, over ravines and viaducts, and gazes imperiously down on the road to   15
Andorra running through valley floors below. But even for this intrepid reporter, who suffers from vertigo, the trip is exhilarating and fun rather than scary.

Villefranche is an impeccably preserved walled town, the fortifications of which were designed by Vauban, the great military engineer of Louis XIV, to withstand the slings and arrows of outrageous neighbours, not to mention cannonballs. It is now a UNESCO World Heritage site,   20 officially categorised as among the most beautiful villages in France, and would be a perfect location for a swashbuckling film. Cue d'Artagnan and his Three Musketeers for action.

The train I board has a choice of four closed and two open-air carriages, all painted bright yellow, and as the sun is beaming from clear blue skies I opt for one of the latter. With a shrill whistle we are off, quickly reaching our cruising speed of about 15mph as we rock and roll past Vauban's battlements.   25

This is the way to travel through tumultuous scenery, at a gentle pace with time to gaze on   27
fast flowing streams, deep forests, and dizzying gorges. Mountain villages are etched on the skyline, clinging to impossible slopes, their church towers like rockets poised to take off for the heavens.   30

The eyes are constantly drawn upwards to forests in the sky, and convoluted valleys snaking up to barren peaks, a grand, sweeping symphony of nature. At times the railway seems to defy gravity, and when we halt there is no rumbling of diesel engines, only silence broken by the rushing of a river below.   34

Seven of the original ten Yellow Train units are still operating, and when one of two modern   35
units pulls up beside us, it is greeted with scorn. 'Look at that,' a fellow passenger remarks. 'It has nothing to do with the history of this railway. I'd sooner take the bus.'

Fortunately he doesn't have to, because with five services daily in each direction it is possible to hop on and off at intermediate stations.

After rattling over France's only railway suspension bridge we climb to Bolquère-Eyne, the   40
country's highest station at 5,226 feet. We have now emerged in Mackintosh's fairyland, a plateau of green fields and meadows framed by distant mountains that seems like the roof of the world.

Mackintosh's destination was Mont Louis, a couple of miles back down the line. It is another of Vauban's impressive fortified villages, which has maintained its military heritage with a   45
commando training centre. There are guided tours of the barracks, where men are schooled in the arts of fighting, blowing things up, and kidnapping people.

It seems like an odd pursuit in fairyland. I prefer Mackintosh's take on it.

Source B: 19th-century non-fiction

This is an extract from a magazine article, 'Railway Imprisonment', published in The Saturday Review of Politics, Literature, Science and Art *in 1864. When trains were first invented, carriages were separate, with no connecting corridor or means of contacting the conductor. The writer discusses some of the problems with this design.*

It is the glory of an age of scientific progress to have invented a perfectly new and unique   1
description of social torture. The English railway carriage may be defined as a machine of
unparalleled efficiency for isolating a human being from the companionship and protection of
his fellow creatures, and exposing him, a helpless prey, to murderous outrage.

It is a prison from which there is no escaping but with the certainty of broken bones and the   5
risk of being pounded to atoms. It is a prison where associates may be forced upon a man
without any choice of his own, of whose character and background he knows nothing, and
who, for all he can tell, may be assassins or lunatics.

No seclusion from the outside world can be more absolute, while it lasts, than that of the
English railway traveller. For an interval varying from a few minutes to an hour or more, you   10
may be shut up with a stranger of sinister features and worse than dubious manner, with the
awareness on both sides that nothing but your physical power of resistance can repel any
unlawful behaviour that evil, lust or frenzy may prompt. You know it, and he knows it, and you
know that he knows it. You might as well be on another planet for any protection that society
has to give you against the foulest of crimes or the most terrible of mortal danger.   15

A few days ago, on the South Western line, a young woman was vilely insulted by a ruffian,
the sole occupant of the compartment besides herself, and only escaped something worse
than insult by throwing open the door and taking refuge on the step, while the train was at
full speed. She would have been dashed to pieces but for the nerve and presence of mind
of a passenger in the adjoining compartment, who seized the poor creature just as she was   20
fainting, and succeeded in holding her for some five miles, until an alarm was given to the
guard by some labourers at work in a field. The thing seems barely credible, and yet, apart
from the melodramatic horror of the situation, it is nothing more than an extreme instance of
what may happen any day to any defenceless girl shut up with an unknown brute. The case
of this young woman, frightened into an act next door to suicide, is only an unusually startling   25

illustration of that helpless exposure to brutality which Railway Boards, in defiance of all warning, persist in making a condition of English travelling.

And the infliction is a perfectly unnecessary one. The Boards themselves have not the nerve to say that this absolute isolation from all human comfort and protection is an unavoidable incident of railway locomotion. Nobody pretends that it is impossible to provide means of communication between passengers and guards. An exterior ledging or platform, attached to each carriage, is all that is needed to enable the guard to pass along the whole length of a train in motion as many times in the course of a journey as may be thought necessary. It is absurdly suggested that this is dangerous, but with the simple accompaniment of a handrail, it is about as dangerous as walking up stairs. This convenient attachment, with the addition of a contrivance for enabling a frightened or insulted passenger to summon the guard to his relief, would furnish, if not absolute security, at all events a tolerably sufficient practical safeguard against nine-tenths of the dangers and annoyances to which the English Railway Boards choose to subject their countrymen.

It is for Parliament and the public to compel the Boards to perform a plain duty which ought to need no compulsion. Railway Companies must be made answerable in damages for the consequences of wilfully leaving their passengers unprotected against foul and murderous violence, just as they are answerable for any other 'accident'.

30

35

40

Section A: Reading

Answer **all** questions in this section.

You are advised to spend about 45 minutes on this section.

| 0 | 1 | Read again the first part of **Source A** from **lines 1 to 6**.

Choose **four** statements below which are **true**.

- Shade the **circles** in the boxes of the ones that you think are **true**.
- Choose a maximum of **four** statements.
- If you make an error cross out the **whole box**.
- If you change your mind and require a statement that has been crossed out then draw a circle around the box.   **[4 marks]**

A   It is quicker to travel by road than rail.   ⬭

B   The writer enjoys travelling by train.   ⬭

C   The train journey begins at a modern French town.   ⬭

D   The town where the train journey begins is in a mountain valley.   ⬭

E   The train climbs up to the mountain peak.   ⬭

F   The train travels through the western Pyrenees.   ⬭

G   The writer thinks the train challenges people's expectations.   ⬭

H   This train route has been running for fewer than 100 years.   ⬭

| 0 | 2 | You need to refer to **Source A** and **Source B** for this question.

Both sources describe specific passengers who are upset.

Use details from **both** sources to write a summary of what you understand about the differences between the specific passengers who are upset.

[8 marks]

| 0 | 3 | You now need to refer only to **Source A** from **lines 27 to 34**.

How does the writer use language to describe the view from the train?

[12 marks]

0 4   For this question, you need to refer to the **whole of Source A**, together with the **whole of Source B**.

Compare how the writers convey their different perspectives on travelling by train.

In your answer, you could:

- compare their different perspectives on travelling by train
- compare the methods the writers use to convey their perspectives
- support your response with references to both texts.

[16 marks]

Section B: Writing

You are advised to spend about 45 minutes on this section.

Write in full sentences.

You are reminded of the need to plan your answer.

You should leave enough time to check your work at the end.

0 5   'Foreign travel is supposed to broaden the mind, but all it really does is cost a fortune and destroy the planet. These days we can see any place we want to on the Internet.'

Write an article for a newspaper in which you argue your point of view on this statement.

(24 marks for content and organisation
16 marks for technical accuracy)

[40 marks]

Preparing to practise

Before you attempt this practice exam paper, it is important to remember which skills are being assessed in each question and what you are expected to do to demonstrate those skills. Read through the following and think about the tips for each question.

Question 1

Example Exam Question

01 Read again the first part of **Source A** from **lines 1 to 6**.

Choose **four** statements which are true.

[4 marks]

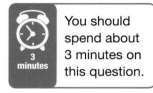

You should spend about 3 minutes on this question.

Skills and objectives

• To identify and interpret explicit and implicit information (AO1)

What you have to do

• Find the four statements that are true out of the given eight statements. In this practice exam paper the true statements will relate to **lines 1 to 6** of **Source A**.

Tips

• Make sure you focus on the correct source.

• Make sure you focus on the correct lines.

• Select the four statements that are true – no more and no less.

• Remember that the given statements are in chronological order. This will help you to focus on the exact words and phrases in the text in order to judge which statements are true and which are false.

Question 2

Example Exam Question

02 You need to refer to **Source A** and **Source B** for this question.

Both sources describe specific passengers who are upset.

Use details from **both** sources to write a summary of what you understand about the differences between the specific passengers who are upset.

[8 marks]

You should spend about 10 minutes on this question.

Skills and objectives

- To identify and interpret explicit and implicit information **(AO1)**
- To select and synthesise evidence from different texts **(AO1)**

What you have to do

- Focus on the given similarity or difference. In this practice exam paper you have to focus on the **differences between the specific passengers who are upset**.

- Identify the appropriate information and ideas in each text. In this practice exam paper you are looking for information and ideas about **the specific passengers who are upset**.

- Make inferences from the individual texts and the similarities/differences between them.

Tips

- Make sure you focus on the given similarity or difference.

- Make sure you write about relevant information and ideas in **both** texts.

- Remember that the most important part of this question is the **quality** of what you write about the **individual texts and the similarities/differences between them**. Your comments have to be **precise** and **contextualised** in order to achieve Level 3 and above.

- Remember to interpret each individual text as well as the similarities/differences between them.

- Support what you say with references from **both** texts.

Key term

contextualise: to analyse a word or phrase in terms of the words or ideas surrounding it

Question 3

Example Exam Question

03 You now need to refer only to **Source A** from **lines 27 to 34**.

How does the writer use language to describe the view from the train?

[12 marks]

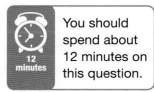

You should spend about 12 minutes on this question.

Skills and objectives

- To analyse how the writer's use of language achieves effects **(AO2)**

What you have to do

- Choose some examples of language. In this practice exam paper you have to focus on language in **lines 27 to 34** of **Source A** used **to describe the view from the train**.

- Write about the effects of your selected examples of language.

- Use subject terminology to enhance your response.

Tips

- Make sure you select examples of language from the correct source.

- Make sure you select examples of language from the correct lines.

- Remember that the most important part of this question is the **quality** of what you write about the effects of language. Your comments have to be **precise** and **contextualised** in order to achieve Level 3 and above.

- Zoom in on individual words and phrases to analyse their effects.

Question 4

Example Exam Question

04 For this question, you need to refer to the **whole of Source A**, together with the **whole of Source B**.

Compare how the writers convey their different perspectives on travelling by train.

In your answer, you could:

- compare their different perspectives on travelling by train
- compare the methods the writers use to convey their perspectives
- support your response with references to both texts.

[16 marks]

You should spend about 20 minutes on this question.

Skills and objectives

- To compare writers' ideas and perspectives, and how these are conveyed **(AO3)**

What you have to do

- Focus on the given statement. In this practice exam paper the focus is **travelling by train**.

- Identify the writer's ideas and perspectives in each text. In this practice exam paper you are looking for the writers' different ideas and perspectives on **travelling by train**.

- Compare the writers' ideas and perspectives in both texts.

- Make inferences from the individual texts and the similarities/ differences between them.

- Comment on the effects of the writers' methods used to convey these ideas and perspectives.

- Support your comparison with textual references.

Tips

- Make sure you write about relevant information and ideas in **both** texts.

- Remember that the most important part of this question is the **quality** of what you write about both **the writers' ideas and perspectives**, and **the methods used to convey these ideas and perspectives**. Your comments have to be **precise** and **contextualised** in order to achieve Level 3 and above.

- Remember to interpret each individual text as well as to compare the similarities/differences between them.

- Include lots of comparison words/phrases, e.g. 'both', 'similarly', 'however', 'whereas', 'on the other hand', 'in contrast', etc.

- Support what you say with references from **both** texts.

Question 5

Example Exam Question

05 'Foreign travel is supposed to broaden the mind, but all it really does is cost a fortune and destroy the planet. These days we can see any place we want to on the Internet.'

Write an article for a newspaper in which you argue your point of view on this statement.

[40 marks]

You should spend about 35 minutes on this question: 5 minutes to plan, 25 minutes to write and 5 minutes to check at the end.

Skills and objectives

- To communicate effectively in an appropriate style according to purpose and audience **(AO5)**
- To organise information and ideas, using structural and grammatical features **(AO5)**
- To write clearly and accurately **(AO6)**

What you have to do

- Produce a piece of discursive writing that communicates to the reader.
- Demonstrate the ability to match tone, style and **register** to purpose and audience.
- **Structure** your writing effectively.
- Engage and convince the reader of your point of view.
- Link and develop your ideas.
- Use effective vocabulary and phrasing.
- Use paragraphs and discourse markers effectively.
- Use effective **linguistic devices**.
- Write accurately.

Tips

- Remember that what is being assessed is the **quality** of your writing. You have to communicate **clearly** in order to reach Level 3 or above.

- Take time to plan your response before you start writing – decide on your point of view, think of two or three main reasons why you hold this point of view and also some counter-arguments so that you can argue against them, and then decide on the tone you want to adopt.

- Consider how to convince your reader using a structured argument, a strong opening and strategies to engage such as the use of opinion, facts and anecdotes.

- Leave time at the end to proofread your response, and correct and improve where possible.

Activity 1: Answering the practice exam paper

Using all the tips you have read above, complete the practice exam paper on pages 62–67.

Using all the tips you have read above, complete the practice exam paper on pages 62–67.

Key terms

linguistic devices: words or phrases that convey meaning which is different to the literal meaning of the words. Those most useful in discursive writing include:

- **fact:** something that you can prove is true.

- **opinion:** something that you believe to be true but it may not be.

- **anecdote:** a short, personal story about something interesting that has happened.

- **statistics:** numbers and figures to support your argument.

- **exaggeration:** to overstate something for effect.

- **pattern of three:** listing three things to create a specific effect.

- **rhetorical question:** a question asked to make a point where no answer is expected.

register: the level of formality used in writing or the language used by a particular group of people

Unpicking the mark scheme

A mark scheme is used to assess the quality of your response for each question. Unpicking the mark scheme can show you how levels and marks are awarded. This can help you to improve the quality of your work because you will understand exactly what is expected of you in each question.

Question 1 mark scheme

Example Exam Question

01 Choose **four** statements which are true.

[4 marks]

Question 1 is different from all the other Reading questions because it is the only question where you are given answers and you have to decide which ones are correct. You are awarded 1 mark for each true statement you select, up to a total of 4 marks.

What follows is the Question 1 mark scheme for the practice exam paper on pages 62–67.

A	It is quicker to travel by road than rail. [T]
B	The writer enjoys travelling by train. [T]
C	The train journey begins at a modern French town. [F]
D	The town where the train journey begins is in a mountain valley. [T]
E	The train climbs up to the mountain peak. [F]
F	The train travels through the western Pyrenees. [F]
G	The writer thinks the train challenges people's expectations. [T]
H	This train route has been running for fewer than 100 years. [F]

Some of the true statements are obvious and are explicitly written in the text. Other statements are implicit and you have to show understanding of the text in order to judge whether or not they are true.

A It is quicker to travel by road than rail. This statement is true because it explicitly says: 'The road to fairyland is quicker…'.

B The writer enjoys travelling by train. This statement is true, and you can work this out from where it says: '… the railway is more fun'.

C The train journey begins at a modern French town. This statement is false, and you can work this out from where it says: 'It begins at a medieval fortified town…'. The word 'medieval' means very old, which is the opposite of modern.

D The town where the train journey begins is in a mountain valley. This statement is true because it explicitly says: '… deep in a French mountain valley'.

E The train climbs up to the mountain peak. This statement is false, and you can work this out from where it says: '… climbs to a plateau in the sky'. The word 'plateau' means level ground, which is the opposite of a peak.

F The train travels through the western Pyrenees. This statement is false because it explicitly says: '… eastern Pyrenees…'.

73

G The writer thinks the train challenges people's expectations. This statement is true, and you can work this out from where it says: 'defying' both 'time and space'. The word 'defying' here means challenging.

H This train route has been running for fewer than 100 years. This statement is false, and you can work this out from where it says: '... for more than a century'. The word 'century' means 100 years.

Improving your Question 1 response

Activity 2: Self-assessment

a. Look again at your original response to Question 1. Decide how many marks you would be awarded at the moment. Use the mark scheme on page 73 to help you make your decision.

b. Find the references given in the guidance on pages 73–74 in the original text to understand any incorrect choices.

c. Rewrite your response with the correct four true statements.

Question 2 mark scheme

Example Exam Question

02 Both **Source A** and **Source B** describe specific passengers who are upset.

Use details from **both** sources to write a summary of what you understand about the differences between the specific passengers who are upset.

[8 marks]

The mark scheme for Question 2 consists of three columns:

- **Level:** There are four levels, from Level 1 at the bottom to Level 4 at the top. Each level has key words that sum up the quality of responses in that level.

Level	Key words	Explanation
Level 4	'Detailed' and 'perceptive'	This means you have identified similarities/differences that are deep below the surface and your interpretation of them is insightful and astute.
Level 3	'Clear' and 'relevant'	This means you have identified clear similarities/differences and your interpretation of them is developed, precise and contextualised.
Level 2	'Some' and 'attempts'	This means you have identified some similarities/differences and are trying to interpret them, but what you are saying is undeveloped and not yet clear.
Level 1	'Simple' and 'limited'	This means you have identified an obvious similarity/difference but failed to offer any interpretation.

- **Skills descriptors:** This column shows the skills being assessed in Question 2. Your response is placed in a level according to how well you have demonstrated the key skill – interpreting the individual texts and the similarities/differences between them. How well you demonstrate the other skills determines your mark within that level.

- **Indicative standard:** This column shows the **quality** of response that is expected at each level. It does not show the correct answer in terms of content because you may not select the same similarities/differences, but the quality of your interpretation will be matched against the quality of these indicative standard responses.

What follows is the Question 2 mark scheme for the practice exam paper on pages 62–67. Because the most important part of this question is the **quality** of what you write about the individual texts and the similarities/differences between them, this key skill has been highlighted so that you can trace the thread through the mark scheme levels to see the progression from Level 1 to Level 4.

> **Key term**
>
> **judicious:** showing considered judgement

Level	Skills descriptors	Indicative standard
Level 4 Detailed, perceptive summary 7–8 marks	Shows perceptive or detailed synthesis and interpretation of both texts: • Makes perceptive inferences from both texts • Makes **judicious** references/use of textual detail relevant to the focus of the question • Shows perceptive differences between texts	Both passengers are upset but to very differing degrees. The man in Source A is merely disgruntled. He is disappointed at the lack of authenticity of some of the Little Yellow Train units, and believes replacing the originals detracts from the 'history of this railway'. He greets the modern unit 'with scorn', suggesting a contempt and disdain that it not really necessary. The woman in Source B, however, is distraught when she is 'vilely insulted by a ruffian', so much so that she seeks sanctuary on the outside step of the carriage while 'the train was at full speed' in case 'something worse than insult' follows. Her choice of potential death over being trapped inside with an 'unknown brute' displays a far more genuine reason for feeling upset.
Level 3 Clear, relevant summary 5–6 marks	Shows clear synthesis and interpretation of both texts: • Makes clear inferences from both texts • Selects clear references/textual detail relevant to the focus of the question • Shows clear differences between texts	Both passengers are upset but the woman in Source B has far more reason. She is 'vilely insulted by a ruffian' and takes refuge on the step outside of the carriage while 'the train was at full speed'. Her actions suggest her upset is so great that she is forced to risk her own life to escape. However, the man in Source A is just upset that not all the train units on the Little Yellow Train are part of the railway's history. When a modern unit pulls up beside him, he 'greets it with scorn', suggesting he is full of contempt because it is not original.

Level	Skills descriptors	Indicative standard
Level 2 Some attempts at summary 3–4 marks	Shows some interpretation from one/both texts: • Attempts some inference(s) from one/both texts • Selects some appropriate references/textual detail from one/both texts • Shows some difference(s) between texts	The passenger in Source A is upset because he sees a train unit that is modern. He says, 'It has nothing to do with the history of this railway', so he doesn't like that it's not real. The upset woman in Source B has more to complain about because she is insulted by a man and escapes onto the step outside of the carriage while the train is going 'at full speed'. Her life is in danger, unlike the man in Source A, who is just grumpy.
Level 1 Simple, limited summary 1–2 marks	Shows simple awareness from one/both texts: • Offers paraphrase rather than inference • Selects simple reference(s)/textual detail(s) from one/both texts • Shows simple difference between texts	The man in Source A is a bit upset because he doesn't like the new train unit. The woman in Source B is different because she is really upset. She stands on the step outside the carriage when someone insults her and nearly dies because the train is going 'at full speed'.

Activity 3: Tracking levels of response

a. To help you see the progression more clearly, choose one comment in the highlighted Level 1 indicative standard response, e.g. 'because he doesn't like the new train unit'. Copy it out, and then write down the improved version of this comment shown at Level 2, Level 3, and Level 4. Look at the quality of comment demonstrated in each level.

b. Think about how you could improve your own response.

Improving your Question 2 response

Activity 4: Self-assessment

a. Look again at your original response to Question 2. Decide which level your response fits into at the moment. Use the mark scheme on pages 75–76 to help you make your decision.

b. Think about which parts of your response you could develop in order to improve it. Look in particular at the **quality** of what you have written about the individual texts and also the differences between them.

- Look at the difference in the skills descriptor bullets at different levels. For example, a response needs to develop from 'attempts some inference(s) from one/both texts' to 'clear inferences from both texts' in order to move from Level 2 to Level 3.

- Work in steps: What appropriate information and ideas have you identified? What inferences can you draw from them? How are these the same/different in the other text?

- The better you link these elements together, the more successful your answer should be.

c. Consider the Upgrade advice in the panel.

d. Rewrite your response with the parts you have developed, and see if you have now achieved a higher mark.

Upgrade

- Find as much evidence as you can about the specific upset passengers in each text.

- Remember to make inferences from the individual texts as well as the differences between them.

- Using a phrase such as 'This suggests...' shows that you are beginning to interpret the differences between the upset passengers. Other useful phrases include: 'This means...', 'This lets us know...', 'This indicates...', 'This implies...' and 'This makes me think...'.

Question 3 mark scheme

Example Exam Question

03 How does the writer use language in **lines 27 to 34 of Source A** to describe the view from the train?

[12 marks]

The mark scheme for Question 3 consists of three columns:

- **Level:** There are four levels, from Level 1 at the bottom to Level 4 at the top. Each level has key words that sum up the quality of responses in that level.

Level	Key words	Explanation
Level 4	'Detailed' and 'perceptive'	This means you are seeing meaning deep below the surface and your analysis of the writer's use of language is insightful and astute.
Level 3	'Clear' and 'relevant'	This means your explanation of the writer's use of language is developed, precise and contextualised.
Level 2	'Some understanding and comment'	This means you are trying to comment on the writer's use of language and you are having some success, but what you are saying is undeveloped and not yet clear.
Level 1	'Simple' and 'limited'	This means what you are saying about the writer's use of language is basic and obvious.

- **Skills descriptors:** This column shows the skills being assessed in Question 3. Your response is placed in a level according to how well you have demonstrated the key skill – writing about the effects of the writer's choice of language. How well you demonstrate the other skills determines your mark within that level.

- **Indicative standard:** This column shows the **quality** of response that is expected at each level. It does not show the correct answer in terms of content because you may not select the same examples of language, but the quality of your analysis of language will be matched against the quality of these indicative standard responses.

What follows is the Question 3 mark scheme for the practice exam paper on pages 62–67. Because the most important part of this question is the **quality** of what you write about the effects of language, this key skill has been highlighted so that you can trace the thread through the mark scheme levels to see the progression from Level 1 to Level 4.

Level	Skills descriptors	Indicative standard
Level 4 Detailed, perceptive analysis 10–12 marks	Shows detailed and perceptive understanding of language: • Analyses the effects of the writer's choices of language • Selects a range of judicious textual detail • Makes sophisticated and accurate use of subject terminology	The simile 'like rockets poised to take off for the heavens' describes the church towers as impressively high – they are so magnificent they appear to be about to propel themselves into the realm of the gods. The writer highlights individual elements of beauty and then summarises them with the metaphor 'a grand, sweeping symphony of nature'. This image portrays the far-reaching majesty of nature as something of a masterpiece of creation when all these scenic elements are blended together.

Level	Skills descriptors	Indicative standard
Level 3 Clear, relevant explanation 7–9 marks	Shows clear understanding of language: • Explains clearly the effects of the writer's choices of language • Selects a range of relevant textual detail • Makes clear and accurate use of subject terminology	The writer uses the simile 'like rockets poised to take off for the heavens' to describe the view of the church towers. This suggests they are so high they look as if they are about to launch themselves into the glorious sky. The overall view is metaphorically described as a 'grand, sweeping symphony of nature', implying the vast expanse of scenery fits together like a perfect work of art.
Level 2 Some understanding and comment 4–6 marks	Shows some understanding of language: • Attempts to comment on the effect of language • Selects some appropriate textual detail • Makes some use of subject terminology, mainly appropriately	The writer can see church towers that are like 'rockets poised to take off'. This simile shows they are huge and pointing up to the sky. He describes the view from the train as a 'grand, sweeping symphony of nature', which suggests it's a big natural space that looks lovely.
Level 1 Simple, limited comment 1–3 marks	Shows simple awareness of language: • Offers simple comment on the effect of language • Selects simple reference(s) or textual detail(s) • Makes simple use of subject terminology, not always appropriately	The writer says the towers of the church are 'like rockets' so they're tall and thin. He describes the view with the words 'grand' and 'sweeping' to show it's big.

Activity 5: Tracking levels of response

a. To help you see the progression more clearly, choose one comment in the highlighted Level 1 indicative standard response, e.g. 'so they're tall and thin'. Copy it out, and then write down the improved version of this comment shown at Level 2, Level 3, and Level 4. Look at the quality of comment demonstrated in each level.

b. Think about how you could improve your own response.

Improving your Question 3 response

Activity 6: Self-assessment

Look again at your original response to Question 3. Decide which level your response fits into at the moment. Use the mark scheme on pages 78–79 to help you make your decision.

a. Think about which parts of your response you could develop in order to improve it. Look in particular at the **quality** of what you have written about the effects of language.

- Look at the difference in the skills descriptor bullets at different levels. For example, a response needs to develop from 'attempts to comment' to 'explains clearly' in order to move from Level 2 to Level 3.

- Work in steps: What word/phrase/language feature have you selected? How has the writer used it to create an effect? Why might the writer have intended this effect?

- The better you link these elements together, the more successful your answer should be.

b. Consider the Upgrade advice in the panel.

c. Rewrite your response with the parts you have developed, and see if you have now achieved a higher mark.

Upgrade

- Think about the effect of the writer's choice of individual words, e.g. 'mountain villages are etched on the skyline'. Why is the word 'etched' particularly successful?

- When discussing the effects of language, remember it is important to consider the context in which the words and phrases are used, and to be precise when commenting on effect.

- Using a phrase such as 'This suggests...' shows that you are beginning to interpret the effect of the writer's language used to describe the view from the train. Other useful phrases include: 'This means...', 'This lets us know...', 'This indicates...', 'This implies...' and 'This makes me think...'.

Question 4 mark scheme

Example Exam Question

04 Refer to the **whole of Source A**, together with the **whole of Source B**.

Compare how the writers convey their different perspectives on travelling by train.

[16 marks]

The mark scheme for Question 4 consists of three columns:

- **Level:** There are four levels, from Level 1 at the bottom to Level 4 at the top. Each level has key words that sum up the quality of responses in that level.

Level	Key words	Explanation
Level 4	'Detailed' and 'perceptive'	This means you are seeing meaning deep below the surface and your comparison of ideas/perspectives and analysis of the writers' methods is insightful and astute.
Level 3	'Clear' and 'relevant'	This means your comparison of ideas/perspectives and explanation of the writers' methods is developed, precise and contextualised.
Level 2	'Some' and 'attempts'	This means you are trying to compare ideas/perspectives and comment on the writers' methods and you are having some success, but what you are saying is undeveloped and not yet clear.
Level 1	'Simple' and 'limited'	This means your comparison of ideas/perspectives and what you are saying about the writers' methods is basic and obvious.

- **Skills descriptors:** This column shows the skills being assessed in Question 4. Your response is placed in a level according to how well you have demonstrated the key skill – writing about both the writers' ideas and perspectives, and the methods used to convey these ideas and perspectives. How well you demonstrate the other skills determines your mark within that level.

- **Indicative standard:** This column shows the **quality** of response that is expected at each level. It does not show the correct answer in terms of content because you may not select the same ideas and perspectives or the same writers' methods, but the quality of your comparison will be matched against the quality of these comments.

What follows is the Question 4 mark scheme for the practice exam paper on pages 62–67. Because the most important part of this question is the **quality** of what you write about both the writers' ideas and perspectives, and the methods used to convey these ideas and perspectives, these key skills have been highlighted so that you can trace the thread through the mark scheme levels to see the progression from Level 1 to Level 4. Green highlighting shows comments on the writer's ideas and perspectives in each source; yellow highlighting shows comments on the writers' methods.

Level	Skills descriptors	Indicative standard
Level 4 Perceptive, detailed comparison 13–16 marks	Compares ideas and perspectives in a perceptive way • Analyses how writers' methods are used • Selects a range of judicious supporting detail from both texts • Shows a detailed and perceptive understanding of the different ideas and perspectives in both texts	Source A is a modern article, written from the perspective of a passenger, describing the positive and 'fun' aspects of travelling by train, whereas Source B, written at a time when the railways were newly invented, is much more negative, possibly because the Victorians were suspicious of something so revolutionary. The writer of Source B highlights the issues with the design of railway carriages – the 'seclusion from the outside world' due to the lack of a connecting corridor or ability to communicate with the guard. His intention is to persuade parliament to make the rail companies solve the issues they are already aware of and choose to ignore. He effectively employs bathos when he says 'It is the glory of an age of scientific progress to have invented a perfectly new and unique description of social torture', his sarcasm suggesting that what was designed to improve humanity has, in fact, diminished it. However, the writer of Source A uses beautiful descriptive language, with an extended metaphor of being spellbound – 'magical trip', 'enchanted' and the repetition of 'fairyland' suggest the writer is enthralled and simply bewitched by rail travel.

Level	Skills descriptors	Indicative standard
Level 3 Clear, relevant comparison 9–12 marks	Compares ideas and perspectives in a clear and relevant way • Explains clearly how writers' methods are used • Selects relevant detail to support from both texts • Shows a clear understanding of the different ideas and perspectives in both texts	Source A is a first-hand account written by a passenger and it is very positive about train travel, calling it 'fun', whereas the Victorian writer of Source B, who is not used to trains, is much more negative. He says the carriages are separate and there is no way for people to reach the guard when the train is moving. Therefore, he is concerned with the potential dangers faced by passengers who could be in a carriage with 'lunatics'. He uses the metaphor of a 'prison' to convey they are trapped with no way out. The writer of Source A is the opposite. He describes his trip as 'magical', suggesting it is so wonderful he feels he is under a spell.
Level 2 Some attempts at comparison 5–8 marks	Attempts to compare ideas and perspectives • Makes some comment on how writers' methods are used • Selects some appropriate textual detail/references, not always supporting, from one or both texts • Shows some understanding of different ideas and perspectives	The writer of Source A is a passenger and is positive about train travel, but the writer of Source B isn't on a train and he doesn't like them. He thinks the carriages aren't built properly because the people inside can't get out once the train is going and they could be stuck with 'lunatics'. He uses emotive language like 'prison' to show they can't get out. The writer of Source A thinks travelling by train is great. He describes it as 'magical' to show how special he thinks it is.
Level 1 Simple, limited comment 1–4 marks	Makes simple cross reference of ideas and perspectives • Makes simple identification of writers' methods • Selects simple reference(s)/textual detail(s) from one or both texts • Shows simple awareness of ideas and/or perspectives	The writer of Source A likes travelling by train but the writer of Source B doesn't. He thinks it's dangerous because you don't know who you're travelling with and they could be 'lunatics'. Source A uses words like 'magical trip', which makes travelling by train sound lovely.

Activity 7: Tracking levels of response

a. To help you see the progression more clearly, choose one comment in the highlighted Level 1 indicative standard response, e.g. 'Source A uses words like "magical trip"...'. Copy it out, and then write down the improved version of this comment shown at Level 2, Level 3, and Level 4. Look at the quality of comment demonstrated in each level.

b. Think about how you could improve your own response.

Improving your Question 4 response

Activity 8: Self-assessment

a. Look again at your original response to Question 4. Decide which level your response fits into at the moment. Use the mark scheme on pages 81–82 to help you make your decision.

b. Think about which parts of your response you could develop in order to improve it. Look in particular at the **quality** of your comparison of the writers' ideas and perspectives, and the methods used to convey these ideas and perspectives.

- Look at the difference in the skills descriptor bullets at different levels. For example, a response needs to develop from 'makes some comment' to 'explains clearly' in order to move from Level 2 to Level 3.

- Work in steps: What relevant ideas and perspectives have you identified to compare? What methods have the writers used to convey those ideas and perspectives?

- The better you link these elements together, the more successful your answer should be.

c. Consider the Upgrade advice in the panel.

d. Rewrite your response with the parts you have developed, and see if you have now achieved a higher mark.

Upgrade

- As part of your comparison, remember you are expected to interpret ideas and perspectives in the individual texts as well as the differences between them.

- Make sure you also comment on the effects of the writers' methods used to convey the ideas and perspectives on travelling by train. In these texts you could consider not only language and structure, but also tone, purpose and **narrative voice**.

- Try to develop an organic structure to the response, making links between points and connections between texts.

Key term

narrative voice: the characteristic ways in which the narrator speaks and thinks

Question 5 mark scheme

Example Exam Question

05 'Foreign travel is supposed to broaden the mind, but all it really does is cost a fortune and destroy the planet. These days we can see any place we want to on the Internet.'

Write an article for a newspaper in which you argue your point of view on this statement.

[40 marks]

In Question 5 you will be assessed on:

- Content and Organisation **(AO5)**

- Technical Accuracy **(AO6)**.

So the mark scheme for Question 5 is divided into two parts.

The mark scheme for Content and Organisation (AO5) consists of three columns:

- **Level:** There are four levels, from Level 1 at the bottom to Level 4 at the top. Each level has key words that sum up the quality of responses in that level.

Level	Key words	Explanation
Level 4	'Compelling, convincing communication'	This means that your writing is crafted for impact. Ideas are linked in a confident, seamless manner and form a unified whole. Your reader is completely convinced by your line of argument.
Level 3	'Consistent, clear communication'	This means that your writing is shaped, fluent and makes sense as a whole. Ideas are effectively linked, developed and relevant to purpose. Your reader can clearly follow your line of argument.
Level 2	'Some successful communication'	This means that your writing makes sense at times. Some ideas are linked but others may be illogical or undeveloped. Your reader can follow your line of argument in parts but sometimes loses the thread of what you are saying.
Level 1	'Simple, limited communication'	This means that your writing doesn't always make sense. Ideas are basic and may be rambling and not well organised. Your reader struggles to follow your line of argument.

- **Sub-level:** Each of the four levels is broken down into an upper level and a lower level. To move into an upper level you have to demonstrate a higher level of skill or sustain the skills in the lower half of the level.

- **Skills descriptors:** This column shows the skills being assessed in Question 5. Your response is placed in a level according to how well you have demonstrated the key skill – overall communication. How well you demonstrate the other skills determines your mark within that level.

What follows is the Question 5 mark scheme for Content and Organisation (AO5) for the practice exam paper on pages 62–67. Because the most important part of this question is the **quality** of your overall communication, this key skill has been highlighted so that you can trace the thread through the mark scheme levels to see the progression from Level 1 to Level 4.

Level	Sub-level	Skills descriptors
Level 4 Compelling, convincing communication 19–24 marks	Upper Level 4 22–24 marks	**Content** • Communication is convincing and compelling • **Tone**, style and **register** are assuredly matched to purpose and audience • Extensive and ambitious vocabulary with sustained crafting of **linguistic devices** **Organisation** • Varied and inventive use of structural features • Writing is compelling, incorporating a range of convincing and complex ideas • Fluently linked paragraphs with seamlessly integrated discourse markers
	Lower Level 4 19–21 marks	**Content** • Communication is convincing • Tone, style and register are convincingly matched to purpose and audience • Extensive vocabulary with conscious crafting of linguistic devices **Organisation** • Varied and effective structural features • Writing is highly engaging with a range of developed complex ideas • Consistently coherent use of paragraphs with integrated discourse markers

Level	Sub-level	Skills descriptors
Level 3 Consistent, clear communication 13–18 marks	Upper Level 3 16–18 marks	**Content** • Communication is consistently clear • Tone, style and register are clearly and consistently matched to purpose and audience • Increasingly sophisticated vocabulary and phrasing, chosen for effect with a range of successful linguistic devices **Organisation** • Effective use of structural features • Writing is engaging, using a range of clear connected ideas • Coherent paragraphs with integrated discourse markers
	Lower Level 3 13–15 marks	**Content** • Communication is generally clear • Tone, style and register are generally matched to purpose and audience • Vocabulary clearly chosen for effect and appropriate use of linguistic devices **Organisation** • Usually effective use of structural features • Writing is engaging, with a range of connected ideas • Usually coherent paragraphs with range of discourse markers
Level 2 Some successful communication 7–12 marks	Upper Level 2 10–12 marks	**Content** • Communicates with some sustained success • Some sustained attempt to match tone, style and register to purpose and audience • Conscious use of vocabulary with some use of linguistic devices **Organisation** • Some use of structural features • Increasing variety of linked and relevant ideas • Some use of paragraphs and some use of discourse markers
	Lower Level 2 7–9 marks	**Content** • Communicates with some success • Attempts to match tone, style and register to purpose and audience • Begins to vary vocabulary with some use of linguistic devices **Organisation** • Attempts to use structural features • Some linked and relevant ideas • Attempts to write in paragraphs with some discourse markers, not always appropriate

Level	Sub-level	Skills descriptors
Level 1 Simple, limited communication 1–6 marks	Upper Level 1 4–6 marks	**Content** • Communicates simply • Simple awareness of matching tone, style and register to purpose and audience • Simple vocabulary; simple linguistic devices **Organisation** • Evidence of simple structural features • One or two relevant ideas, simply linked • Random paragraph structure
	Lower Level 1 1–3 marks	**Content** • Limited communication • Occasional sense of matching tone, style and register to purpose and audience • Simple vocabulary **Organisation** • Limited or no evidence of structural features • One or two unlinked ideas • No paragraphs

The mark scheme for Technical Accuracy (AO6) consists of two columns:

• **Level:** There are four levels, from Level 1 at the bottom to Level 4 at the top.

Level	Explanation
Level 4	At this level your writing is extremely accurate. Spelling, punctuation and grammar are almost faultless, and sentences are crafted for impact.
Level 3	At this level your writing is generally accurate. Spelling, punctuation and grammar are mostly secure, and sentences are successfully varied for effect.
Level 2	At this level your writing is sometimes accurate. Spelling, punctuation and grammar contain some errors and sentences are varied for effect but with mixed success.
Level 1	At this level your writing is not very accurate. Spelling, punctuation and grammar contain basic errors and sentences lack variety.

What follows is the Question 5 mark scheme for Technical Accuracy (AO6) for the practice exam paper on pages 62–67.

Level	Skills descriptors
Level 4 13–16 marks	• **Sentence demarcation** is consistently secure and consistently accurate • Wide range of punctuation is used with a high level of accuracy • Uses a full range of appropriate **sentence forms** for effect • Uses **Standard English** consistently and appropriately with secure control of complex **grammatical structures** • High level of accuracy in spelling, including ambitious vocabulary • Extensive and ambitious use of vocabulary
Level 3 9–12 marks	• Sentence demarcation is mostly secure and mostly accurate • Range of punctuation is used, mostly with success • Uses a variety of sentence forms for effect • Mostly uses Standard English appropriately with mostly controlled grammatical structures • Generally accurate spelling, including complex and **irregular words** • Increasingly sophisticated use of vocabulary
Level 2 5–8 marks	• Sentence demarcation is mostly secure and sometimes accurate • Some control of a range of punctuation • Attempts a variety of sentence forms • Some use of Standard English with some control of agreement • Some accurate spelling of more complex words • Varied use of vocabulary
Level 1 1–4 marks	• Occasional use of sentence demarcation • Some evidence of conscious punctuation • Simple range of sentence forms • Occasional use of Standard English with limited control of agreement • Accurate basic spelling • Simple use of vocabulary

Key terms

grammatical structure: the arrangement of words, phrases, clauses and sentences to make correct grammatical sense

irregular word: a word that does not follow spelling or phonic 'rules'

sentence demarcation: writing sentences correctly using capital letters and end punctuation, e.g. full stops, question marks and exclamation marks

sentence forms: single-clause and multi-clause sentence types such as simple, complex and compound

Standard English: the form of English language widely accepted as the usual correct form, especially in formal or public situations

Improving your Question 5 response

Activity 9: Self-assessment

a. Look again at your original response to Question 5. Decide which Content and Organisation (AO5) level your response fits into at the moment based on the overall **quality** of your writing. Use the mark scheme on pages 85–87 to help you make your decision.

b. Think about which parts of your response you could develop in order to improve the Content and Organisation (AO5). Look in particular at how well you have demonstrated your ability to:

   • match tone, style and register to purpose and audience
   • structure your writing effectively
   • engage and convince the reader of your point of view
   • link and develop your ideas
   • use effective vocabulary and phrasing
   • use paragraphs and discourse markers effectively.
   • use effective linguistic devices.

c. Consider the Upgrade advice in the panel.

d. Now decide which Technical Accuracy (AO6) level your response fits into at the moment based on how accurately it is written. Use the mark scheme on page 88 to help you make your decision.

e. Think about which parts of your response could be improved in terms of Technical Accuracy (AO6). Look in particular at how well you have demonstrated your ability to:

   • use accurate spelling
   • use accurate punctuation
   • use accurate grammar
   • vary your sentences effectively.

f. Consider the Upgrade advice in the panel.

g. Rewrite your response with the parts you have developed, corrected and improved, and see if you have now achieved a higher mark.

Upgrade

AO6
Remember, effective communication is the most important skill. If you make too many mistakes in spelling, punctuation and grammar, you will not be able to communicate your ideas effectively.

Upgrade

AO5

• When considering how to improve your newspaper article, make sure you are clear about your point of view, the two or three main reasons why you hold this point of view, your counter-arguments to argue against and also the tone you want to adopt.

• Remember your line of argument should be convincing, and include strategies to engage your reader, such as the use of opinion, facts and anecdotes.

• Remember to start your newspaper article in a way that captures your reader's interest immediately.

Progress check

Now you have revisited your original practice exam paper, you are in a position to see which questions you feel confident about and which still need improvement. Look back at the 'What you have to do' sections on pages 68–72 to remind yourself of the skills you need to demonstrate in each question. Then complete the progress check below.

Question 1

	I am confident in this skill.	I have some confidence in this skill.	I need more practice in this skill.
I can find the four statements that are true out of the given eight statements.			

Question 2

	I am confident in this skill.	I have some confidence in this skill.	I need more practice in this skill.
I can focus on the given similarity or difference.			
I can identify the appropriate information and ideas in each text.			
I can make inferences from the individual texts and the similarities/differences between them.			

Question 3

	I am confident in this skill.	I have some confidence in this skill.	I need more practice in this skill.
I can choose some examples of language.			
I can write about the effects of my selected examples of language.			
I can use subject terminology to enhance my response.			

Question 4

	I am confident in this skill.	I have some confidence in this skill.	I need more practice in this skill.
I can identify the writer's ideas and perspectives in each text.			
I can compare the writers' ideas and perspectives in both texts.			
I can make inferences from the individual texts and the similarities/differences between them.			
I can comment on the effects of the writer's methods used to convey these ideas and perspectives.			
I can support my evaluation with textual references.			
I can focus on the given statement.			

Question 5

	I am confident in this skill.	I have some confidence in this skill.	I need more practice in this skill.
I can produce a piece of discursive writing that communicates to the reader.			
I can match tone, style and register to purpose and audience.			
I can structure my writing effectively.			
I can link and develop my ideas.			
I can use effective vocabulary and phrasing.			
I can use paragraphs and discourse markers effectively.			
I can use effective linguistic devices.			
I can spell accurately.			
I can use punctuation accurately.			
I can use grammar accurately.			
I can vary my sentences effectively.			

Chapter 4: Sample exam paper 2

Source A: 21st-century literary non-fiction

This is an extract from a non-fiction book, The Old Ways: A Journey on Foot *by Robert Macfarlane, published in 2012. Macfarlane is a writer who is fascinated by nature. In this extract, he describes a walk through the countryside on a winter's evening.*

Two days short of the winter solstice; the turn of the year's tide. All that cold day, the city and the countryside around felt halted, paused. Five degrees below freezing and the earth battened down. Clouds held snow that would not fall. Out in the suburbs the schools were closed, people homebound, the pavements **rinky** and the roads black-iced. The sun ran a shallow arc across the sky. Then just before dusk the snow came – dropping straight for five hours and settling at a steady inch an hour. 1

5
6

I was at my desk that evening, trying to work but distracted by the weather. I kept stopping, standing, looking out of the window. The snow was sinking through the orange cone cast by a street light, the fat flakes showing like furnace sparks.

Around eight o'clock the snow ceased. An hour later I went for a walk with a flask of whisky to keep me warm. I walked for half a mile along dark back roads where the snow lay clean and unmarked. The houses began to thin out. A few undrawn curtains: family evenings underway, the flicker and burble of television sets. The cold like a wire in the nose. A slew of stars, the moon flooding everything with silver. 10

At the southerly fringe of the suburb, a last lamp post stands by a hawthorne hedge, and next to it is a hole in the hedge which leads down to a modest field path. 15

I followed the field path east-south-east towards a long chalk hilltop, visible as a whaleback in the darkness. Northwards was the glow of the city, and the red blip of aircraft warning lights from towers and cranes. Dry snow squeaked underfoot. A fox crossed the field to my west at a trot. The moonlight was so bright that everything cast a crisp moon-shadow: black on white, stark as woodcut. Wands of dogwood made zebra-hide of the path; hawthorn threw a lattice. The trees were frilled with snow, which lay to the depth of an inch or more on branches and twigs. The snow caused everything to exceed itself and the moonlight caused everything to double itself. 17

20

This is the path I've probably walked more often than any other in my life. It's a young way;   25
maybe fifty years old, no more. Its easterly hedge is mostly hawthorn and around eight feet
high; its westerly hedge is a younger mix of blackthorn, hawthorn, hazel and dogwood. It is not
normally a beautiful place, but there's a feeling of secrecy to it that I appreciate, hedged in as it
is on both sides, and running discretely as it does between field and road. In summer I've seen   29
small rolling clouds of goldfinches rising from teasel-heads and then curling ahead to settle   30
again, retreating in the measure that I approach them.

That evening the path was a grey snow alley, and I followed it up to the hanger of beech trees
that tops the whaleback hill, passing off the clay and onto the chalk proper. At the back brink
of the beech wood I ducked through an ivy-trailed gap, and was into the forty-acre field that
lies beyond.   35

At first sight the field seemed flawless. Then I set out across it and started to see the signs. The
snow was densely printed with the tracks of birds and animals – archives of the hundreds of
journeys made since the snow had stopped. There were neat deer slots, partridge prints like
arrowheads pointing the way, and the pads of rabbits. Lines of tracks curved away from me
across the field, disappearing into shadow or hedge. The moonlight, falling at a slant, deepened   40
the dark in the nearer tracks so that they appeared full as inkwells. To all these marks I added
my own.

The snow was overwhelmingly legible. Each print-trail seemed like a plot that could be read
backwards in time; a series of allusions to events since ended. I found a line of fox **pugs**, which
here and there had been swept across by the fox's brush, as if it had been trying to erase   45
evidence of its own passage. I discovered what I supposed were the traces of a pheasant
taking off: trenched footprints where it had pushed up, then spaced feather-presses either side
of the tracks, becoming progressively lighter and then vanishing altogether.

I chose to follow a deer's trail, which angled tightly across a corner of the field. The slots
led through a blackthorn hedge: I snagged my way after them and emerged into a surreal   50
landscape.

Glossary: **rinky:** slippery
                pugs: prints

Source B: 19th-century non-fiction

This is an extract from a magazine article, 'The Pageant of Summer' by Richard Jefferies, published in Longman's Magazine *in 1883. Jefferies was a Victorian writer who was also fascinated by nature. In this extract, he discusses the effect of summertime on the countryside.*

As the wind, wandering over the sea, takes from each wave an invisible portion, and brings   1
to those on shore the essence of ocean, so the air lingering among the woods and hedges
becomes full of fine atoms of summer. Sweeping from jagged hawthorn leaves, broad-
topped oak leaves, narrow ash sprays and sharp-taloned brambles; brushing from the waving
grasses and stiffening corn, the dust of the sunshine is borne along and breathed. Steeped   5
in flower and pollen to the music of bees and birds, the stream of the atmosphere becomes
a living thing. It is life to breathe it, for the air itself is life. The strength of the earth goes
up through the leaves into the wind, and our hearts open to the width and depth of the
summer – to the broad horizon afar, down to the minutest creature in the grass, up to the
highest swallow.
                                                                                                 10
Winter shows us matter in its dead form, like the rocks, like granite – clear but cold and
frozen. Summer shows us matter changing into life, sap rising from the earth through a million
tubes, the power of light entering the solid oak; and see, it bursts forth in countless leaves!
Living things leap in the grass; living things drift upon the air; living things come forth to
breathe in every hawthorn bush. No longer does the immense weight of matter – the dead,   15
the **crystallised** winter – press ponderously on the thinking mind. The whole purpose of
matter is to feed life – to feed the green rushes, and the roses that are about to be; to feed the
swallows above, and us that wander beneath them.

Fanning so swiftly, the wasp's wings are but just visible as he passes; if he paused, the
light would be apparent through their texture. On the wings of the dragonfly as he hovers   20
an instant before he darts, there is a **prismatic** gleam. These wing textures are even more
delicate than the minute **filaments** on a swallow's feather, more delicate than the pollen of
a flower. They are formed of matter indeed, but how exquisitely it is resolved into the means
and organs of life!

Though not often consciously recognised, perhaps this is the great pleasure of summer, to   25
watch the earth, the dead particles, resolving themselves into living examples of life, to see
the seed-leaf push aside the earth and become by degrees the perfumed flower. From the

tiny mottled egg come the birds' wings that by and by shall cross the immense sea. It is in this marvellous transformation of earth and cold matter into living things that the joy and the hope of summer reside. 30

Every blade of grass, each leaf, each separate floret and petal, is an inscription speaking of hope. Consider the grasses and the oaks, the swallows, the sweet blue butterfly – they are one and all a sign and token showing before our eyes earth made into life. So that my hope becomes as broad as the horizon afar, reiterated by every leaf, sung on every bough, reflected in the gleam of every flower. There is so much for us yet to come, so much to be gathered, 35 and enjoyed.

Not only for you and me, now, but for our race, who, I believe, will ultimately use this magical secret for their happiness. Earth holds secrets enough to give them the life of the fabled Immortals. My heart is fixed firm and stable in the belief that ultimately the sunshine and the summer, the flowers and the azure sky, shall become, as it were, interwoven into man's 40 existence. He shall take from all their beauty and enjoy their glory. Hence it is that a flower is to me so much more than stalk and petals.

Glossary: **crystallised:** frozen solid
prismatic: many colours caused by shining light
filaments: slender, thread-like fibres

Section A: Reading

Answer **all** questions in this section.

You are advised to spend about 45 minutes on this section.

0 1 Read again the first part of **Source A** from **lines 1 to 6**.

Choose **four** statements below which are true.

- Shade the **circles** in the boxes of the ones that you think are **true**.
- Choose a maximum of **four** statements.
- If you make an error cross out the **whole box**.
- If you change your mind and require a statement that has been crossed out then draw a circle around the box.

[4 marks]

A The winter solstice had passed.

B The temperature was five degrees below freezing.

C The earth prepared for what was to come.

D Snow fell all day.

E Schools stayed open despite the cold weather.

F The roads were covered in an ice that was almost invisible.

G The snow fell after dusk.

H The snow settled at a constant rate.

0 2 You need to refer to **Source A** and **Source B** for this question.

Both sources describe creatures in the countryside.

Use details from **both** sources to write a summary of what you understand about the differences between the creatures.

[8 marks]

0 3 You now need to refer only to **Source A** from **lines 17 to 29**.

How does the writer use language to describe what he sees while walking along the field path?

[12 marks]

0 4   For this question, you need to refer to the **whole of Source A**, together with the **whole of Source B**.

Compare how the writers convey their different perspectives on nature.

In your answer, you could:

- compare their different perspectives on nature
- compare the methods the writers use to convey their perspectives
- support your response with references to both texts.

[16 marks]

Section B: Writing

You are advised to spend about 45 minutes on this section.

Write in full sentences.

You are reminded of the need to plan your answer.

You should leave enough time to check your work at the end.

0 5   'Peace and quiet, fresh air and the people are friendlier – living in the countryside has everything needed for a perfect life.'

Write an article for a lifestyle magazine which persuades readers for or against the view that living in the countryside is perfect.

(24 marks for content and organisation
16 marks for technical accuracy)

[40 marks]

Preparing to practise

Before you attempt this practice exam paper, it is important to remember which skills are being assessed in each question and what you are expected to do to demonstrate those skills. Read through the following and think about the tips for each question.

Question 1

Example Exam Question

01 Read again the first part of **Source A** from **lines 1 to 6**.

Choose **four** statements which are true.

[4 marks]

 You should spend about 3 minutes on this question.

Skills and objectives

- To identify and interpret explicit and implicit information **(AO1)**

What you have to do

- Find the four statements that are true out of the given eight statements. In this practice exam paper the true statements will relate to **lines 1 to 6** of **Source A**.

Tips

- Make sure you focus on the correct source.

- Make sure you focus on the correct lines.

- Select the four statements that are true – no more and no less.

- Remember that the given statements are in chronological order. This will help you to focus on the exact words and phrases in the text in order to judge which statements are true and which are false.

Question 2

Example Exam Question

02 You need to refer to **Source A** and **Source B** for this question.

Both sources describe creatures in the countryside.

Use details from **both** sources to write a summary of what you understand about the differences between the creatures.

[8 marks]

You should spend about 10 minutes on this question.

Skills and objectives

- To identify and interpret explicit and implicit information **(AO1)**
- To select and synthesise evidence from different texts **(AO1)**

What you have to do

- Focus on the given similarity or difference. In this practice exam paper you have to focus on the **differences between the creatures in the countryside.**

- Identify the appropriate information and ideas in each text. In this practice exam paper you are looking for information and ideas about **the creatures**.

- Make inferences from the individual texts and the similarities/ differences between them.

Tips

- Make sure you focus on the given similarity or difference.

- Make sure you write about relevant information and ideas in **both** texts.

- Remember that the most important part of this question is the **quality** of what you write about the **individual texts and the similarities/differences between them**. Your comments have to be **precise** and **contextualised** in order to achieve Level 3 and above.

- Remember to interpret each individual text as well as the similarities/differences between them.

- Support what you say with references from **both** texts.

Question 3

Example Exam Question

03 You now need to refer only to **Source A** from **lines 17 to 29**.

How does the writer use language to describe what he sees while walking along the field path?

[12 marks]

You should spend about 12 minutes on this question.

Skills and objectives

• To analyse how the writer's use of language achieves effects **(AO2)**

What you have to do

• Choose some examples of language. In this practice exam paper you have to focus on language in **lines 17 to 29** of **Source A** used **to describe what the writer sees while walking along the field path**.

• Write about the effects of your selected examples of language.

• Use subject terminology to enhance your response.

Tips

• Make sure you select examples of language from the correct source.

• Make sure you select examples of language from the correct lines.

• Remember that the most important part of this question is the **quality** of what you write about the effects of language. Your comments have to be **precise** and **contextualised** in order to achieve Level 3 and above.

• Zoom in on individual words and phrases to analyse their effects.

Question 4

Example Exam Question

04 For this question, you need to refer to the **whole of Source A**, together with the **whole of Source B**.

Compare how the writers convey their different perspectives on nature.

In your answer, you could:

- compare their different perspectives on nature

- compare the methods the writers use to convey their perspectives

- support your response with references to both texts.

[16 marks]

You should spend about 20 minutes on this question.

Skills and objectives

- To compare writers' ideas and perspectives, and how these are conveyed **(AO3)**

What you have to do

- Focus on the given statement. In this practice exam paper the focus is **nature**.

- Identify the writer's ideas and perspectives in each text. In this practice exam paper you are looking for the writers' different ideas and perspectives on **nature**.

- Compare the writers' ideas and perspectives in both texts.

- Make inferences from the individual texts and the similarities/differences between them.

- Comment on the effects of the writers' methods used to convey these ideas and perspectives.

- Support your comparison with textual references.

Tips

- Make sure you write about relevant information and ideas in **both** texts.

- Remember that the most important part of this question is the **quality** of what you write about both **the writers' ideas and perspectives,** and **the methods used to convey these ideas and perspectives**. Your comments have to be **precise** and **contextualised** in order to achieve Level 3 and above.

- Remember to interpret each individual text as well as to compare the similarities/differences between them.

- Include lots of comparison words/phrases, e.g. 'both', 'similarly', 'however', 'whereas', 'on the other hand', 'in contrast', etc.

- Support what you say with references from **both** texts.

Question 5

Example Exam Question

05 'Peace and quiet, fresh air and the people are friendlier – living in the countryside has everything needed for a perfect life.'

Write an article for a lifestyle magazine which persuades readers for or against the view that living in the countryside is perfect.

[40 marks]

You should spend about 35 minutes on this question: 5 minutes to plan, 25 minutes to write and 5 minutes to check at the end.

Skills and objectives

- To communicate effectively in an appropriate style according to purpose and audience **(AO5)**
- To organise information and ideas, using structural and grammatical features **(AO5)**
- To write clearly and accurately **(AO6)**

What you have to do

- Produce a piece of discursive writing that communicates to the reader.
- Demonstrate the ability to match tone, style and register to purpose and audience.
- Structure your writing effectively.
- Engage and convince the reader of your point of view.
- Link and develop your ideas.
- Use effective vocabulary and phrasing.
- Use paragraphs and discourse markers effectively.
- Use effective linguistic devices.
- Write accurately.

Tips

- Remember that what is being assessed is the **quality** of your writing. You have to communicate **clearly** in order to reach Level 3 or above.

- Take time to plan your response before you start writing – decide on your point of view, think of two or three main reasons why you hold this point of view and also some counter-arguments so that you can argue against them, and then decide on the tone you want to adopt.

- Consider how to convince your reader using a structured argument, a strong opening and strategies to engage such as the use of opinion, facts and anecdotes.

- Leave time at the end to proofread your response, and correct and improve where possible.

Activity 1: Answering the practice exam paper

Using all the tips you have read above, complete the practice exam paper on pages 92–97.

Unpicking the mark scheme

A mark scheme is used to assess the quality of your response for each question. Unpicking the mark scheme can show you how levels and marks are awarded. This can help you to improve the quality of your work because you will understand exactly what is expected of you in each question.

Question 1 mark scheme

Example Exam Question

01 Choose **four** statements which are true.   **[4 marks]**

Question 1 is different from all the other Reading questions because it is the only question where you are given answers and you have to decide which ones are correct. You are awarded 1 mark for each true statement you select, up to a total of 4 marks.

What follows is the Question 1 mark scheme for the practice exam paper on pages 92–97.

> **A** The winter solstice had passed. [F]
> **B** The temperature was five degrees below freezing. [T]
> **C** The earth prepared for what was to come. [T]
> **D** Snow fell all day. [F]
> **E** Schools stayed open despite the cold weather. [F]
> **F** The roads were covered in an ice that was almost invisible. [T]
> **G** The snow fell after dusk. [F]
> **H** The snow settled at a constant rate. [T]

Some of the true statements are obvious and are explicitly written in the text. Other statements are implicit and you have to show understanding of the text in order to judge whether or not they are true.

A The winter solstice had passed. This statement is false, and you can work this out from where it says: 'Two days short of the winter solstice...'. The phrase 'short of' means less than or, in this sentence, before, which is the opposite of passed.

B The temperature was five degrees below freezing. This statement is true because it explicitly says: 'Five degrees below freezing...'.

C The earth prepared for what was to come. This statement is true, and you can work this out from where it says: '... the earth battened down'. The phrase 'battened down' here means prepared for heavy snow.

D Snow fell all day. This statement is false because it explicitly says: 'Clouds held snow that would not fall...'.

E Schools stayed open despite the cold weather. This statement is false because it explicitly says: '... the schools were closed'.

F The roads were covered in an ice that was almost invisible. This statement is true, and you can work this out from where it says: '... and the roads black-iced'. Black ice is a thin coating of clear ice on a surface that makes it difficult to see.

G The snow fell after dusk. This statement is false because it explicitly says: '... just before dusk'.

H The snow settled at a constant rate. This statement is true, and you can work this out from where it says: '... settling at a steady inch an hour'. The word 'steady' means regular and constant.

Improving your Question 1 response

Activity 2: Self-assessment

a. Look again at your original response to Question 1. Decide how many marks you would be awarded at the moment. Use the mark scheme on page 103 to help you make your decision.

b. Find the references given in the guidance on pages 103–104 in the original text to understand any incorrect choices.

c. Rewrite your response with the correct four true statements.

Question 2 mark scheme

Example Exam Question

02 Both **Source A** and **Source B** describe creatures in the countryside.

Use details from **both** sources to write a summary of what you understand about the differences between the creatures.

[8 marks]

The mark scheme for Question 2 consists of three columns:

- **Level:** There are four levels, from Level 1 at the bottom to Level 4 at the top. Each level has key words that sum up the quality of responses in that level.

Level	Key words	Explanation
Level 4	'Detailed' and 'perceptive'	This means you have identified similarities/differences that are deep below the surface and your interpretation of them is insightful and astute.
Level 3	'Clear' and 'relevant'	This means you have identified clear similarities/differences and your interpretation of them is developed, precise and contextualised.
Level 2	'Some' and 'attempts'	This means you have identified some similarities/differences and are trying to interpret them, but what you are saying is undeveloped and not yet clear.
Level 1	'Simple' and 'limited'	This means you have identified an obvious similarity/difference but failed to offer any interpretation.

- **Skills descriptors:** This column shows the skills being assessed in Question 2. Your response is placed in a level according to how well you have demonstrated the key skill – interpreting the individual texts and the similarities/differences between them. How well you demonstrate the other skills determines your mark within that level.

- **Indicative standard:** This column shows the **quality** of response that is expected at each level. It does not show the correct answer in terms of content because you may not select the same similarities/differences, but the quality of your interpretation will be matched against the quality of these indicative standard responses.

What follows is the Question 2 mark scheme for the practice exam paper on pages 92–97. Because the most important part of this question is the **quality** of what you write about the individual texts and the similarities/ differences between them, this key skill has been highlighted so that you can trace the thread through the mark scheme levels to see the progression from Level 1 to Level 4.

Level	Skills descriptors	Indicative standard
Level 4 Detailed, perceptive summary 7–8 marks	Shows perceptive or detailed synthesis and interpretation of both texts: • Makes perceptive inferences from both texts • Makes judicious references/use of textual detail relevant to the focus of the question • Shows perceptive differences between texts	Both sources describe very different creatures found in the countryside in different seasons and times of the day. The wintertime 'birds and animals' in Source A are only apparent from the 'lines of tracks' in the snow, and the observation that the fox's prints are almost covered over, 'as if it had been trying to erase evidence of its own passage', suggests a seemingly deliberate motivation by the creatures to remain hidden in their secret nocturnal world where man does not belong. However, Source B focuses on summertime insects, especially the wasp, although the fact that 'the wasp's wings are but just visible as he passes' suggests a glimpse that is only fleeting, and therefore the wasp is possibly as elusive as the creatures in Source A.
Level 3 Clear, relevant summary 5–6 marks	Shows clear synthesis and interpretation of both texts: • Makes clear inferences from both texts • Selects clear references/ textual detail relevant to the focus of the question • Shows clear differences between texts	Both sources describe creatures in the countryside but in Source A they are 'birds and animals' that come out at night in winter and in Source B they are summertime insects. The only evidence in Source A is the 'lines of tracks' in the snow. The fox's prints are almost covered over, 'as if it had been trying to erase evidence of its own passage', which suggests the creatures are deliberately hiding in their own night-time world. However, in Source B, the wasp is actually seen, although only briefly: 'the wasp's wings are but just visible as he passes'. This suggests the insects are more visible to people as they are not nocturnal.

Level	Skills descriptors	Indicative standard
Level 2 Some attempts at summary 3–4 marks	Shows some interpretation from one/both texts: • Attempts some inference(s) from one/both texts • Selects some appropriate references/textual detail from one/both texts • Shows some difference(s) between texts	In Source A the creatures described are 'birds and animals' that come out at night. Only their tracks are seen in the snow, so it might be that they are hiding from the humans. However, in Source B the creatures are insects like wasps and dragonflies. These are different because they are out in the daytime in summer. It says 'the wasp's wings are but just visible as he passes', so people do get to see it but only for a while.
Level 1 Simple, limited summary 1–2 marks	Shows simple awareness from one/both texts: • Offers paraphrase rather than inference • Selects simple reference(s)/textual detail(s) from one/both texts • Shows simple difference between texts	Source A describes 'birds and animals', such as deer, partridge, rabbits, fox and pheasant, but in Source B the creatures are insects. The birds and animals leave tracks in the snow, which show they have been there, but the insects just fly by.

Activity 3: Tracking levels of response

a. To help you see the progression more clearly, choose one comment in the highlighted Level 1 indicative standard response, e.g. 'which show they have been there'. Copy it out, and then write down the improved version of this comment shown at Level 2, Level 3, and Level 4. Look at the quality of comment demonstrated in each level.

b. Think about how you could improve your own response.

Improving your Question 2 response

Activity 4: Self-assessment

a. Look again at your original response to Question 2. Decide which level your response fits into at the moment. Use the mark scheme on pages 105–106 to help you make your decision.

b. Think about which parts of your response you could develop in order to improve it. Look in particular at the **quality** of what you have written about the individual texts and also the differences between them.

- Look at the difference in the skills descriptor bullets at different levels. For example, a response needs to develop from 'attempts some inference(s) from one/both texts' to 'clear inferences from both texts' in order to move from Level 2 to Level 3.

- Work in steps: What appropriate information and ideas have you identified? What inferences can you draw from them? How are these the same/different in the other text?

- The better you link these elements together, the more successful your answer should be.

c. Consider the Upgrade advice in the panel.

d. Rewrite your response with the parts you have developed, and see if you have now achieved a higher mark.

Upgrade

- Find as much evidence as you can about the creatures in the countryside in each text.

- Remember to make inferences from the individual texts as well as the differences between them.

- Using a phrase such as 'This suggests...' shows that you are beginning to interpret the differences between the creatures. Other useful phrases include: 'This means...', 'This lets us know...', 'This indicates...', 'This implies...' and 'This makes me think...'.

Question 3 mark scheme

Example Exam Question

03 How does the writer use language in **lines 17 to 29 of Source A** to describe what he sees while walking along the field path?

[12 marks]

The mark scheme for Question 3 consists of three columns:

- **Level:** There are four levels, from Level 1 at the bottom to Level 4 at the top. Each level has key words that sum up the quality of responses in that level.

Level	Key words	Explanation
Level 4	'Detailed' and 'perceptive'	This means you are seeing meaning deep below the surface and your analysis of the writer's use of language is insightful and astute.
Level 3	'Clear' and 'relevant'	This means your explanation of the writer's use of language is developed, precise and contextualised.
Level 2	'Some understanding and comment'	This means you are trying to comment on the writer's use of language and you are having some success, but what you are saying is undeveloped and not yet clear.
Level 1	'Simple' and 'limited'	This means what you are saying about the writer's use of language is basic and obvious.

- **Skills descriptors:** This column shows the skills being assessed in Question 3. Your response is placed in a level according to how well you have demonstrated the key skill – writing about the effects of the writer's choice of language. How well you demonstrate the other skills determines your mark within that level.

- **Indicative standard:** This column shows the **quality** of response that is expected at each level. It does not show the correct answer in terms of content because you may not select the same examples of language, but the quality of your analysis of language will be matched against the quality of these indicative standard responses.

What follows is the Question 3 mark scheme for the practice exam paper on pages 92–97. Because the most important part of this question is the **quality** of what you write about the effects of language, this key skill has been highlighted so that you can trace the thread through the mark scheme levels to see the progression from Level 1 to Level 4.

Level	Skills descriptors	Indicative standard
Level 4 Detailed, perceptive analysis 10–12 marks	Shows detailed and perceptive understanding of language: • Analyses the effects of the writer's choices of language • Selects a range of judicious textual detail • Makes sophisticated and accurate use of subject terminology	The writer uses an extended metaphor of monochrome colours to convey the effect of the moonlight on the countryside. He says the bright moon 'cast a crisp moon shadow', the sharp alliteration highlighting the definitive contrast of the silhouetted trees against the whiteness of firm snow on a freezing cold night. The path then resembles 'zebra-hide', an image where the juxtaposition of black and white shadows has created perfection by recreating the stripes of one of nature's miracles.

Level	Skills descriptors	Indicative standard
Level 3 Clear, relevant explanation 7–9 marks	Shows clear understanding of language: • Explains clearly the effects of the writer's choices of language • Selects a range of relevant textual detail • Makes clear and accurate use of subject terminology	The writer sees the moon 'cast a crisp moon shadow: black on white'. The word 'crisp' suggests that the black tree shapes on the white snow are distinct and clear-cut in the freezing cold. This idea is developed with the metaphor 'wands of dogwood made zebra-hide of the path', showing the black and white striped patterns are definite, striking and also beautiful.
Level 2 Some understanding and comment 4–6 marks	Shows some understanding of language: • Attempts to comment on the effect of language • Selects some appropriate textual detail • Makes some use of subject terminology, mainly appropriately	The writer sees a 'crisp moon shadow: black and white'. This tells us it is a cold night and the light of the moon is creating black tree shapes on the white snow. He also describes the trees making a 'zebra-hide of the path'. This metaphor suggests the shadows on the ground are black and white striped.
Level 1 Simple, limited comment 1–3 marks	Shows simple awareness of language: • Offers simple comment on the effect of language • Selects simple reference(s) or textual detail(s) • Makes simple use of subject terminology, not always appropriately	The writer sees a 'crisp moon shadow', which shows the moon is out and making shadows. He uses the word 'zebra-hide' to describe the path, so it's black and white like a zebra.

Activity 5: Tracking levels of response

a. To help you see the progression more clearly, choose one comment in the highlighted Level 1 indicative standard response, e.g. 'so it's black and white like a zebra'. Copy it out, and then write down the improved version of this comment shown at Level 2, Level 3, and Level 4. Look at the quality of comment demonstrated in each level.

b. Think about how you could improve your own response.

Improving your Question 3 response

Activity 6: Self-assessment

a. Look again at your original response to Question 3. Decide which level your response fits into at the moment. Use the mark scheme on pages 108–109 to help you make your decision.

b. Think about which parts of your response you could develop in order to improve it. Look in particular at the **quality** of what you have written about the effects of language.

- Look at the difference in the skills descriptor bullets at different levels. For example, a response needs to develop from 'attempts to comment' to 'explains clearly' in order to move from Level 2 to Level 3.

- Work in steps: What word/phrase/language feature have you selected? How has the writer used it to create an effect? Why might the writer have intended this effect?

- The better you link these elements together, the more successful your answer should be.

c. Consider the Upgrade advice in the panel.

d. Rewrite your response with the parts you have developed, and see if you have now achieved a higher mark.

Upgrade

- Think about the effect of the writer's choice of individual words, e.g. 'The trees were frilled with snow'. Why is the word 'frilled' particularly successful?

- When discussing the effects of language, remember it is important to consider the context in which the words and phrases are used, and to be precise when commenting on effect.

- Using a phrase such as 'This suggests...' shows that you are beginning to interpret the effect of the writer's language used to describe what he sees while walking along the field path.

Question 4 mark scheme

Example Exam Question

04 Refer to the **whole of Source A**, together with the **whole of Source B**.

Compare how the writers convey their different perspectives on nature.

[16 marks]

The mark scheme for Question 4 consists of three columns:

- **Level:** There are four levels, from Level 1 at the bottom to Level 4 at the top. Each level has key words that sum up the quality of responses in that level.

Level	Key words	Explanation
Level 4	'Detailed' and 'perceptive'	This means you are seeing meaning deep below the surface and your comparison of ideas/perspectives and analysis of the writers' methods is insightful and astute.
Level 3	'Clear' and 'relevant'	This means your comparison of ideas/perspectives and explanation of the writers' methods is developed, precise and contextualised.
Level 2	'Some' and 'attempts'	This means you are trying to compare ideas/perspectives and comment on the writers' methods and you are having some success, but what you are saying is undeveloped and not yet clear.
Level 1	'Simple' and 'limited'	This means your comparison of ideas/perspectives and what you are saying about the writers' methods is basic and obvious.

- **Skills descriptors:** This column shows the skills being assessed in Question 4. Your response is placed in a level according to how well you have demonstrated the key skill – writing about both the writers' ideas and perspectives, and the methods used to convey these ideas and perspectives. How well you demonstrate the other skills determines your mark within that level.

- **Indicative standard:** This column shows the **quality** of response that is expected at each level. It does not show the correct answer in terms of content because you may not select the same ideas and perspectives or the same writers' methods, but the quality of your comparison will be matched against the quality of these comments.

What follows is the Question 4 mark scheme for the practice exam paper on pages 92–97. Because the most important part of this question is the **quality** of what you write about both the writers' ideas and perspectives, and the methods used to convey these ideas and perspectives, these key skills have been highlighted so that you can trace the thread through the mark scheme levels to see the progression from Level 1 to Level 4. Green highlighting shows comments on the writer's ideas and perspectives in both sources; yellow highlighting shows comments on the writers' methods.

Level	Skills descriptors	Indicative standard
Level 4 Perceptive, detailed comparison 13–16 marks	Compares ideas and perspectives in a perceptive way • Analyses how writers' methods are used • Selects a range of judicious supporting detail from both texts • Shows a detailed and perceptive understanding of the different ideas and perspectives in both texts	In Source A, Macfarlane presents a particular perspective on nature – the pleasure of observing the countryside first-hand, whereas Jefferies in Source B offers a universal argument on the life-giving properties of summer for mankind. Macfarlane focuses most on tracking animals and is fascinated that 'each print-trail seemed like a plot... a series of allusions to events since ended', suggesting the prints hint at a sequence of events that create an enchanting fairytale of the animals' adventures in the woods that night. However, Jefferies' perspective is totally different. To him, 'the dead, the crystallised winter' is inferior to summer, when every aspect of nature comes alive. He believes a 'marvellous transformation of earth' occurs and the world is reborn. He goes beyond things he can actually see to become more philosophical when he states that every aspect of nature 'is an inscription speaking of hope', and his argument then becomes conceptualised. His heart is 'fixed firm and stable' that summertime will eventually be 'interwoven into man's existence' because the Earth's 'secrets' can offer 'the life of the fabled Immortals', possibly suggesting the restorative properties of the sun can benefit mankind not just spiritually but also physically.

Level	Skills descriptors	Indicative standard
Level 3 Clear, relevant comparison 9–12 marks	Compares ideas and perspectives in a clear and relevant way • Explains clearly how writers' methods are used • Selects relevant detail to support from both texts • Shows a clear understanding of the different ideas and perspectives in both texts	In Source A, Macfarlane is personally walking in the winter countryside and appreciating nature first-hand. Source B is written from a different angle because Jefferies is discussing the benefits of nature for everyone. Macfarlane is particularly interested in tracking animal prints in the snow, and says 'each print-trail seemed like a plot that could be read backwards in time', suggesting the prints could be reversed to tell the story of the creatures' wanderings that night. However, Jefferies sees no life in 'the dead, the crystallised winter' and believes summer is when everything in nature comes alive. He describes it as a 'marvellous transformation of earth', and also becomes quite philosophical because he thinks that with new life comes hope.
Level 2 Some attempts at comparison 5–8 marks	Attempts to compare ideas and perspectives • Makes some comment on how writers' methods are used • Selects some appropriate textual detail/references, not always supporting, from one or both texts • Shows some understanding of different ideas and perspectives	In Source A, Macfarlane writes in the first person about nature because he is out walking in winter, but Jefferies in Source B isn't personally there and it's different because he talks about summer. Macfarlane likes tracking animals and says 'each print-trail seemed like a plot', so it sounds like the prints are telling him a story about the animals. Jefferies doesn't like winter, though, and calls it 'the dead, the crystallised winter'. He thinks things start to grow in summer, so summer is better because there's a 'marvellous transformation'.
Level 1 Simple, limited comment 1–4 marks	Makes simple cross reference of ideas and perspectives • Makes simple identification of writers' methods • Selects simple reference(s)/textual detail(s) from one or both texts • Shows simple awareness of ideas and/or perspectives	Macfarlane in Source A likes winter and writes as if he's there but Jefferies in Source B only likes summer. Macfarlane likes tracking animals in the snow because 'each print-trail seemed like a plot'. Source B is more about what happens in summer when things in nature start to grow.

Activity 7: Tracking levels of response

a. To help you see the progression more clearly, choose one comment in the highlighted Level 1 indicative standard response, e.g. 'writes as if he's there'. Copy it out, and then write down the improved version of this comment shown at Level 2, Level 3, and Level 4. Look at the quality of comment demonstrated in each level.

b. Think about how you could improve your own response.

Improving your Question 4 response

Activity 8: Self-assessment

a. Look again at your original response to Question 4. Decide which level your response fits into at the moment. Use the mark scheme on pages 111–112 to help you make your decision.

b. Think about which parts of your response you could develop in order to improve it. Look in particular at the **quality** of your comparison of the writers' ideas and perspectives, and the methods used to convey these ideas and perspectives.

- Look at the difference in the skills descriptor bullets at different levels. For example, a response needs to develop from 'makes some comment' to 'explains clearly' in order to move from Level 2 to Level 3.

- Work in steps: What relevant ideas and perspectives have you identified to compare? What methods have the writers used to convey those ideas and perspectives?

- The better you link these elements together, the more successful your answer should be.

c. Consider the Upgrade advice in the panel.

d. Rewrite your response with the parts you have developed, and see if you have now achieved a higher mark.

Upgrade

- As part of your comparison, remember you are expected to interpret ideas and perspectives in the individual texts as well as the differences between them.

- Make sure you also comment on the effects of the writers' methods used to convey the ideas and perspectives on nature. In these texts you could consider not only language and structure but also tone, purpose and narrative voice.

- Try to develop an organic structure to the response, making links between points and connections between texts.

Question 5 mark scheme

Example Exam Question

05 'Peace and quiet, fresh air and the people are friendlier – living in the countryside has everything needed for a perfect life.'

Write an article for a lifestyle magazine which persuades readers for or against the view that living in the countryside is perfect.

[40 marks]

In Question 5 you will be assessed on:

- Content and Organisation (**AO5**)
- Technical Accuracy (**AO6**).

So the mark scheme for Question 5 is divided into two parts.

The mark scheme for Content and Organisation (AO5) consists of three columns:

- **Level:** There are four levels, from Level 1 at the bottom to Level 4 at the top. Each level has key words that sum up the quality of responses in that level.

Level	Key words	Explanation
Level 4	'Compelling, convincing communication'	This means that your writing is crafted for impact. Ideas are linked in a confident, seamless manner and form a unified whole. Your reader is completely convinced by your line of argument.
Level 3	'Consistent, clear communication'	This means that your writing is shaped, fluent and makes sense as a whole. Ideas are effectively linked, developed and relevant to purpose. Your reader can clearly follow your line of argument.
Level 2	'Some successful communication'	This means that your writing makes sense at times. Some ideas are linked but others may be illogical or undeveloped. Your reader can follow your line of argument in parts but sometimes loses the thread of what you are saying.
Level 1	'Simple, limited communication'	This means that your writing doesn't always make sense. Ideas are basic and may be rambling and not well organised. Your reader struggles to follow your line of argument.

- **Sub-level:** Each of the four levels is broken down into an upper level and a lower level. To move into an upper level you have to demonstrate a higher level of skill or sustain the skills in the lower half of the level.

- **Skills descriptors:** This column shows the skills being assessed in Question 5. Your response is placed in a level according to how well you have demonstrated the key skill – overall communication. How well you demonstrate the other skills determines your mark within that level.

What follows is the Question 5 mark scheme for Content and Organisation (AO5) for the practice exam paper on pages 92–97. Because the most important part of this question is the **quality** of your overall communication, this key skill has been highlighted so that you can trace the thread through the mark scheme levels to see the progression from Level 1 to Level 4.

Level	Sub-level	Skills descriptors
Level 4 Compelling, convincing communication 19–24 marks	Upper Level 4 22–24 marks	**Content** • Communication is convincing and compelling • Tone, style and register are assuredly matched to purpose and audience • Extensive and ambitious vocabulary with sustained crafting of linguistic devices **Organisation** • Varied and inventive use of structural features • Writing is compelling, incorporating a range of convincing and complex ideas • Fluently linked paragraphs with seamlessly integrated discourse markers
	Lower Level 4 19–21 marks	**Content** • Communication is convincing • Tone, style and register are convincingly matched to purpose and audience • Extensive vocabulary with conscious crafting of linguistic devices **Organisation** • Varied and effective structural features • Writing is highly engaging with a range of developed complex ideas • Consistently coherent use of paragraphs with integrated discourse markers
Level 3 Consistent, clear communication 13–18 marks	Upper Level 3 16–18 marks	**Content** • Communication is consistently clear • Tone, style and register are clearly and consistently matched to purpose and audience • Increasingly sophisticated vocabulary and phrasing, chosen for effect with a range of successful linguistic devices **Organisation** • Effective use of structural features • Writing is engaging, using a range of clear connected ideas • Coherent paragraphs with integrated discourse markers
	Lower Level 3 13–15 marks	**Content** • Communication is generally clear • Tone, style and register are generally matched to purpose and audience • Vocabulary clearly chosen for effect and appropriate use of linguistic devices **Organisation** • Usually effective use of structural features • Writing is engaging, with a range of connected ideas • Usually coherent paragraphs with range of discourse markers

Level	Sub-level	Skills descriptors
Level 2 Some successful communication 7–12 marks	Upper Level 2 10–12 marks	**Content** • Communicates with some sustained success • Some sustained attempt to match tone, style and register to purpose and audience • Conscious use of vocabulary with some use of linguistic devices **Organisation** • Some use of structural features • Increasing variety of linked and relevant ideas • Some use of paragraphs and some use of discourse markers
	Lower Level 2 7–9 marks	**Content** • Communicates with some success • Attempts to match tone, style and register to purpose and audience • Begins to vary vocabulary with some use of linguistic devices **Organisation** • Attempts to use structural features • Some linked and relevant ideas • Attempts to write in paragraphs with some discourse markers, not always appropriate
Level 1 Simple, limited communication 1–6 marks	Upper Level 1 4–6 marks	**Content** • Communicates simply • Simple awareness of matching tone, style and register to purpose and audience • Simple vocabulary; simple linguistic devices **Organisation** • Evidence of simple structural features • One or two relevant ideas, simply linked • Random paragraph structure
	Lower Level 1 1–3 marks	**Content** • Limited communication • Occasional sense of matching tone, style and register to purpose and audience • Simple vocabulary **Organisation** • Limited or no evidence of structural features • One or two unlinked ideas • No paragraphs

The mark scheme for Technical Accuracy (AO6) consists of two columns:

• **Level:** There are four levels, from Level 1 at the bottom to Level 4 at the top.

Level	Explanation
Level 4	At this level your writing is extremely accurate. Spelling, punctuation and grammar are almost faultless, and sentences are crafted for impact.
Level 3	At this level your writing is generally accurate. Spelling, punctuation and grammar are mostly secure, and sentences are successfully varied for effect.
Level 2	At this level your writing is sometimes accurate. Spelling, punctuation and grammar contain some errors and sentences are varied for effect but with mixed success.
Level 1	At this level your writing is not very accurate. Spelling, punctuation and grammar contain basic errors and sentences lack variety.

What follows is the Question 5 mark scheme for Technical Accuracy (AO6) for the practice exam paper on pages 92–97.

Level	Skills descriptors
Level 4 13–16 marks	• Sentence demarcation is consistently secure and consistently accurate • Wide range of punctuation is used with a high level of accuracy • Uses a full range of appropriate sentence forms for effect • Uses Standard English consistently and appropriately with secure control of complex grammatical structures • High level of accuracy in spelling, including ambitious vocabulary • Extensive and ambitious use of vocabulary
Level 3 9–12 marks	• Sentence demarcation is mostly secure and mostly accurate • Range of punctuation is used, mostly with success • Uses a variety of sentence forms for effect • Mostly uses Standard English appropriately with mostly controlled grammatical structures • Generally accurate spelling, including complex and irregular words • Increasingly sophisticated use of vocabulary
Level 2 5–8 marks	• Sentence demarcation is mostly secure and sometimes accurate • Some control of a range of punctuation • Attempts a variety of sentence forms • Some use of Standard English with some control of agreement • Some accurate spelling of more complex words • Varied use of vocabulary
Level 1 1–4 marks	• Occasional use of sentence demarcation • Some evidence of conscious punctuation • Simple range of sentence forms • Occasional use of Standard English with limited control of agreement • Accurate basic spelling • Simple use of vocabulary

Improving your Question 5 response

Activity 9: Self-assessment

a. Look again at your original response to Question 5. Decide which Content and Organisation (AO5) level your response fits into at the moment based on the overall **quality** of your writing. Use the mark scheme on pages 115–116 to help you make your decision.

b. Think about which parts of your response you could develop in order to improve the Content and Organisation (AO5). Look in particular at how well you have demonstrated your ability to:

- match tone, style and register to purpose and audience
- structure your writing effectively
- engage and convince the reader of your point of view
- link and develop your ideas
- use effective vocabulary and phrasing
- use paragraphs and discourse markers effectively
- use effective linguistic devices.

c. Consider the Upgrade advice in the panel.

d. Now decide which Technical Accuracy (AO6) level your response fits into at the moment based on how accurately it is written. Use the mark scheme on page 117 to help you make your decision.

e. Think about which parts of your response could be improved in terms of Technical Accuracy (AO6). Look in particular at how well you have demonstrated your ability to:

- use accurate spelling
- use accurate punctuation
- use accurate grammar
- vary your sentences effectively.

f. Consider the Upgrade advice in the panel.

g. Rewrite your response with the parts you have developed, corrected and improved, and see if you have now achieved a higher mark.

Progress check

Now you have revisited your original practice exam paper, you are in a position to see which questions you feel confident about and which still need improvement. Look back at the 'What you have to do' sections on pages 98–102 to remind yourself of the skills you need to demonstrate in each question. Then complete the progress check below.

Question 1

	I am confident in this skill.	I have some confidence in this skill.	I need more practice in this skill.
I can find the four statements that are true out of the given eight statements.			

Question 2

	I am confident in this skill.	I have some confidence in this skill.	I need more practice in this skill.
I can focus on the given similarity or difference.			
I can identify the appropriate information and ideas in each text.			
I can make inferences from the individual texts and the similarities/differences between them.			

Question 3

	I am confident in this skill.	I have some confidence in this skill.	I need more practice in this skill.
I can choose some examples of language.			
I can write about the effects of my selected examples of language.			
I can use subject terminology to enhance my response.			

Question 4

	I am confident in this skill.	I have some confidence in this skill.	I need more practice in this skill.
I can identify the writer's ideas and perspectives in each text.			
I can compare the writers' ideas and perspectives in both texts.			
I can make inferences from the individual texts and the similarities/differences between them.			
I can comment on the effects of the writer's methods used to convey these ideas and perspectives.			
I can support my evaluation with textual references.			
I can focus on the given statement.			

Question 5

	I am confident in this skill.	I have some confidence in this skill.	I need more practice in this skill.
I can produce a piece of discursive writing that communicates to the reader.			
I can match tone, style and register to purpose and audience.			
I can structure my writing effectively.			
I can link and develop my ideas.			
I can use effective vocabulary and phrasing.			
I can use paragraphs and discourse markers effectively.			
I can use effective linguistic devices.			
I can spell accurately.			
I can use punctuation accurately.			
I can use grammar accurately.			
I can vary my sentences effectively.			